REVISED SECOND EDITION

CHOOSING SMALL

JOB SEARCH STRATEGIES FOR LAWYERS IN THE SMALL FIRM MARKET

CHOOSING SMART

BY DONNA GERSON, ESQ.

D1557564

Featuring advice
"In Their Own Words"
from practitioners and
career counselors

THE ASSOCIATION
FOR LEGAL CAREER
PROFESSIONALS

1025 Connecticut Avenue NW, Suite 1100
Washington, DC 20036-5413
(202) 835-1001 — Fax (202) 835-1112

Website: www.nalp.org

ISBN: 1-55733-044-1

Cover design: Harold Behar, Behar-Fingal

Contents

 # Preface

One in every five law school graduates who enters private practice can expect to begin his or her career in a small law firm or in solo practice. Recent employment statistics from **NALP — The Association for Legal Career Professionals** — indicate that small firm practice is one of the most likely destinations for law school graduates today. Yet few resources address the tremendous range of issues confronting law students and graduates aspiring to join the ranks of the small firm or solo practitioner. This book offers readers comprehensive information about understanding the small firm market and how to approach firms effectively, and strategies for negotiating the best salary and benefits package with your employer, succeeding as an associate at a small firm, and looking beyond small firm practice.

Extensive interviews with small firm practitioners around the country, as well as law school career services directors and bar association professionals, offer you a unique insight into the mind of the small firm practitioner and the hiring process. Using the information provided in this book, you can conquer the small firm market, decipher the hiring timelines, provide relevant information to prospective employers, interview effectively, and flourish as a new attorney in a small firm environment.

Many people contributed words of advice and I thank them all for taking the time to contribute their wisdom and experience.

Thank you to Janet Smith and to NALP for their assistance and encouragement on this project.

Last, but not least, to David and Sam — none of this would be possible without you.

— *Donna Gerson*

CHAPTER 1:

Anatomy of a Small Law Firm

"Knowing what you want is the first step toward getting it."

— MAE WEST

Do you want to learn how to find a job with a small law firm? Think you have what it takes? If you are committed to learning the ropes, then begin unlocking the secrets of a successful job search by understanding the anatomy of a small law firm.

Understanding what constitutes a small firm is the first step to realizing success in your job search. Too often, law students and recent graduates approach the job search process with a hazy, ill-defined sense of what they are seeking. This often results in a frustrating and drawn-out job search. By beginning with some important statistical information, you will gain a better understanding of the small firm market and its intricacies. A sophisticated job seeker — one who understands the market — is always more efficient, productive, and goal-oriented.

According to the most recent statistics collected by the American Bar Foundation, 74% of all lawyers work in private practice. Of those lawyers working in private

➡ Why Choose a Small Firm?

Small, medium, or large? National, regional, or local? Law firms are not "one-size-fits-all." In choosing a law firm, size and structure are important considerations, especially since they often dictate other significant factors such as practice areas, types of clients, billable hours requirements, compensation, partnership opportunities, and how decisions and policies are made.

Smaller and more local firms usually represent smaller or middle-market clients in smaller, less complex matters simply because they do not have the "critical mass" to staff the larger engagements. These firms can have a general practice, similar to the larger firms, or a specialized "boutique" practice. For attorneys who are entrepreneurial or enjoy managing the business of law practice, a smaller, more local practice may be a good fit. Advantages include a more intimate working environment, control over and responsibility for business development and lawyering strategy, more "hands-on" legal experience earlier in one's career, and a chance to be a "big fish in a small pond." Although compensation at smaller firms typically is less, there may be more flexibility with regard to billing rates and arrangements that gives attorneys greater latitude in business development. With a smaller or more local firm, there can be more flexibility in hiring criteria as well. While many such firms still emphasize academic standing, other factors such as demonstrated excellence in a practice specialty or a substantial client base may mitigate a less than stellar academic record.

Valerie Fontaine, Partner
Seltzer Fontaine Beckwith Legal Search Consultants
Los Angeles, California

practice, 66% work in firms of fewer than 50 lawyers. In fact, only 12% of all private practitioners work in firms of more than 100 lawyers. National statistics from NALP for the Class of 2003 indicate that of those graduates entering private practice, 20.3% secured employment with firms of 50 or fewer attorneys. Only 15.1% of the Class of 2003 obtained jobs in mega-firms of more than 500 attorneys.

These statistics demonstrate the demographic reality of law practice in the United States today: most private practitioners work in small or solo environments. If you have chosen to pursue a career in private practice, it's likely that you will find yourself working for a small law firm or a sole practitioner.

Definitions

For the purposes of this book, *small firm* will be defined as a firm with 50 or fewer lawyers. The term "small" will, however, vary with where you reside geographically. The definition of small will be very different for a lawyer in New York City than for a practitioner in a rural Pennsylvania county. A *sole practitioner* is defined as a lawyer practicing on his or her own.

Small firms, like their larger firm counterparts, will vary in the scope and variety of their practices. From a job search perspective, it is important to know the practice areas in which a small firm might specialize because this will influence your entire approach to that firm, from cover letter to interview.

Many small law firms are general practice businesses, doing a little bit of everything from civil litigation to commercial contracts to minor criminal matters. Other law firms will be specialty boutiques handling only a discrete practice area. *Boutique law firms,* as the name implies, engage in a very specific practice area. You will find boutique firms with every practice focus imaginable. Some common examples of boutique practices include intellectual property law, family law, trusts and estates, criminal defense, and entertainment law.

This book does not address the issue of large firms (firms with 100 or more lawyers) with small branch offices. While these branch offices may technically be small, they remain part of a larger law firm organization and hire associates using the same credentials requirements and timetable as large firms. When researching small firms, job seekers need to recognize small branch offices of larger firms and treat them accordingly. Small branch offices of large law firms do not relax their hiring standards and often participate in the fall on-campus interview process at most law schools.

Within law firms, you will find a variety of players, all vital to the economic success of the enterprise. *Partners* are generally lawyers with an ownership interest in the business. *Associates* are lawyers who are employees of the business. Most full-time entry-level positions are for associates. *Paralegals* are professionals who are not licensed to practice law but who serve on a paraprofessional level by organizing and categorizing information, corresponding with clients, and supervising discrete aspects of cases. *Law clerks* hold part-time or full-time positions and are paid on an hourly basis to work on specific issues or cases. Typically, law clerks are law students or recent graduates.

➡ Why I Enjoy Small Firm Practice

I enjoy working in a small firm because the time demands are not as great, so I can be a professional without devoting my whole life to the firm. The pay is not as substantial in a small firm, but the reward of getting to spend a decent portion of your life elsewhere is a more than adequate trade-off.

Small firm practice has also allowed me to develop a depth of knowledge in my practice area that I doubt that I would have gained otherwise. I am one of two attorneys in a practice group, and that means I take cases from start to finish; I don't just prepare files for someone else to take over. That makes life more interesting and also provides me with challenges that make me a better practitioner.

To prepare for small firm employment, one thing you most assuredly need is some kind of background in residential real estate. This is hard (if not impossible) to gain through coursework, but clerking or paralegal work is a good way to get that knowledge. Many of your potential future clients will want you to handle their home purchases and sales, and they will not be happy if you tell them you can't do so. Also, as many small firms devote a fairly significant portion of their practices to residential real estate, having some background will make you more marketable to them.

Anne M. Dobson
Florance, Gordon & Brown
Richmond, Virginia

The Business of Practicing Law

Before you can begin to understand how a small law firm hires, you need to learn about law firm economics. Too many law students approach the job search with a rosy view of hiring that is out of context with the reality of the profession. Law schools do a wonderful job of teaching students about discrete practice areas. Careful attention is paid to the "Rule Against Perpetuities," but little time is spent teaching the nuts and bolts of the business of law. Some students graduate without ever having seen a timesheet or contemplated the importance of knowing how to attract clients. In order to understand small firm hiring, you need to learn about the economics of law firm practice today.

First and foremost, law is both a learned profession *and a business*. Everyone agrees that lawyers are members of a learned profession in that they need to complete an arduous graduate school course of study, take and pass a state bar licensing examination, and (in most jurisdictions) take continuing legal education courses throughout their professional lives. Lawyers are thinkers, analysts, writers, and communicators. They are officers of the court and serve as foundations to a society forged by principles of justice under law. It all sounds very lofty, doesn't it?

Most law students fail to take into account that law is also a business, a way to make a living. The business of law — to use a term of art coined by Edward Poll — dictates how hiring is conducted, why certain candidates are more attractive than other candidates, and ways you can improve your chances of getting on a small firm's radar screen for purposes of being hired.

Lawyers make money by selling their knowledge and expertise in order to solve complex problems for clients. Since valuing "knowledge" and "expertise" is inherently difficult, and because clients typically prefer some objective measure of what the lawyer has been doing, the practice of billing clients for the time lawyers spend has evolved — and has gained nearly universal acceptance in recent years. Billing policies vary from firm to firm. Many firms bill for time spent on cases or deals (called "matters") and both partners and associates complete timesheets describing how they spent their day (usually in increments of 6 to 15 minutes). In other instances, most particularly with plaintiffs' personal injury firms, clients pay based on a contingent fee basis — that is, based on how much money is won. Contingent fees will vary from state to state, but typically run about one-third of the award, minus costs. Even in firms that collect contingent fees, however, lawyers keep track of their time to provide partners with some economic basis on which to evaluate their investment in a case.

Successful law firms make money by being very proficient at their work, bringing in paying clients, and collecting fees in a timely manner. Paying clients are the fuel that runs the law firm engine. Therefore, acquiring client-getting skills (or even expressing an interest in the business side of the practice) will garner positive attention from a small firm employer.

Why Practice at a Small Firm?

Why work at a small firm? You will hear different reasons depending on who answers the question. Here are some reasons to consider working for a small firm:

- **More Responsibility at an Earlier Stage of Your Career**

  Because a small firm has fewer layers of management and generally less ability to staff cases with several tiers of partners, associates, and paralegals, lawyers at small firms are often compelled to assume higher levels of responsibility more quickly than do lawyers in more hierarchical environments. This can be exhilarating for some people and extraordinarily stressful for others. It isn't unusual for entry-level lawyers who work at small firms and have passed the bar to begin handling cases almost immediately with a minimum of supervision.

- **More Client Contact**

  Going hand-in-hand with more responsibility at an earlier stage in your career, you will probably find that you enjoy more client contact as well. Rather than receiving information through several layers of management, legal problems will be conveyed to you more directly, perhaps directly from the client.

- **Potential for Quicker Advancement and Monetary Rewards**

  While you should not expect to earn a mega-firm salary when you begin at a small law firm, many small firms provide the potential for a quicker partnership track and significant monetary rewards. Many large firms are committed to lock-step promotions and salary increases. Smaller firms, by contrast, enjoy the flexibility (and sometimes the profitability) to reward excellence earlier with partnership and monetary rewards. At some personal injury firms, it is not unusual for associates to share in the success of a big win and to take home substantial year-end bonuses in excess of their large firm peers. Practice varies widely from firm to firm, and you are well advised not to make generalized assumptions about the upside potential of small firm life. In Chapter Four, we will discuss compensation issues and suggestions for negotiating salary in greater detail.

- **Incentives for Client-Getting**

Since a few paying clients more or less can make all the difference in a small firm, an associate with an entrepreneurial flair for bringing in business will often be rewarded for doing so. Client-getting, also known as rainmaking, is essential to the success of the business. Without paying clients, the law firm will fail. Incentives for bringing in business will vary from firm to firm. In some cases, associates are rewarded with a percentage of the fee collected. In other cases, flat fees might be given for successful rainmaking.

- **Greater Collegiality**

In the best of all possible worlds, a small firm can be a close-knit group embarked on a common mission: to practice law, assist clients, and be fairly paid for services rendered. Small firms might also enjoy some of the David versus Goliath myth, an "us versus them" mentality engendered by being part of a small team of professionals. Of course, the extent to which greater collegiality actually exists will differ from small firm to small firm. You need to gauge the level of collegiality at the firm based upon your sense at the interview and through the reputation of the firm in the legal community.

The Downside of Small Firm Practice

Small firm practice may not appeal to everyone and you should be aware of some drawbacks, such as:

● **Life in a Fishbowl**

You are unlikely to find a tremendous network of peers within a small firm. In fact, you may be the only associate employed by the firm. If you do not get along with everyone at the firm (including the secretarial staff), then you may find small firm life uncomfortable. This may be particularly true if the partner who supervises you turns out to be unpleasant or, worse, unprofessional.

To that end, use the interview process and other resources at your disposal to conduct a thorough investigation of the firm and its reputation before agreeing to begin work.

- **Solitude**

Larger firms offer the opportunity for you to socialize with peers and participate in professional training sessions. Smaller firms cannot offer these sorts of diversions; thus, you may be the lone associate working long hours. If you are the sort of person who needs to have lots of friendly interactions during the work day and a social life based on work acquaintances, a small firm may not be a good place for you.

- **Performance Pressures**

Since small firms are typically thinly staffed, an entry-level associate is usually expected to handle cases and matters almost immediately with minimal training. Some lawyers describe training as being "thrown to the wolves." Signing your name to a pleading or handling a deposition by yourself is not for the faint of heart. If you are the type of person who craves supervision, mentoring, and instruction, small firm life might be stressful.

- **Salary and Perks**

Most small law firms cannot afford to pay big firm starting salaries, nor can they provide many of the pricey perks such as summer bar review stipends or lavish holiday parties. However, small firms might be willing to reward performance with year-end bonuses or other perks based on your success at the firm.

When Small Firms Hire

Small firms hire when — and only when — they perceive a specific need. Unlike larger law firms, there is no "hiring season" for the small firm lawyer. The ad hoc hiring practices of smaller firms result directly from their business model. Small firms cannot afford to employ underutilized resources; a single lawyer with nothing to do but a salary that the firm must nonetheless pay could mean the difference between profitability and failure. Thus, small firms seek to match resources precisely with demand, without excessive layers of administration and staff. As a result, smaller firms cannot project hiring needs far in advance and will hire when the need arises.

In contrast, larger law firms tend to hire on a more predictable schedule because they know that attrition history (the rate at which lawyers leave the firm for other opportunities) and recurring client needs necessitate entry-level hiring at regular intervals. Larger firms can generally survive having one associate too many, or one too few, at least over the short term. Thus, you'll notice that most of the employers who participate in fall on-campus interviews at your law school are larger firms, who are in effect hiring associates two years in advance.

The lack of a specific small firm hiring season can work to your advantage, because you can approach small firms right now and ascertain their hiring needs. There are two ways to approach firms: reactively and proactively. *Reactive* job searching relies on your reflexes: you wait for jobs to be posted through your career services office or through bar publications. The *proactive* job searcher creates an individual plan through self-reflection, independent research, and networking. This proactive approach gives you far more control over your destiny and will be our focus throughout this book.

If you approach small firms proactively by gathering information, writing to the firms, and making follow-up telephone calls, be prepared to make several different approaches. Due to the unique nature of small firm hiring, it might be the case that a firm is not contemplating hiring in September of your final year of law school but will wind up conducting interviews in March based upon changed circumstances. Because of the shifting nature of most small firm hiring, I recommend that students apply to small law firms several different times during the year — for example, in October, February, and May.

Small firm practice is not for everyone. If you are a person who thrives on lots of responsibility, possesses an entrepreneurial spirit, manifests a strong interest in the day-to-day practice of law, and combines all of that with an interest in learning the business of law, then small firm practice is probably a good path to pursue. If you want to learn how to gather information about small firms and contact them regarding job opportunities, then read on.

➡ When One Small Firm Hires

We are a boutique family law firm in Dallas, Texas, with three partners. Our firm looks for associates when the workload becomes too great, but, more importantly, we need an associate to justify his or her salary/benefits economically. We can always put in extra work to get us through busy times, but if the work is not steady, then we cannot justify hiring a full-time associate. Grades are not particularly important to us, although we would hesitate to hire a prospective associate who had poor grades. In interviewing potential hires, we look primarily for self-starters who display versatility.

Jimmy L. Verner, Jr.
Verner & Brumley, P.C.
Dallas, Texas

CHAPTER 2:

Contacting Small Firms

*"Opportunity is missed by most people
because it is dressed in overalls
and looks like work."*

THOMAS ALVA EDISON

Establishing Parameters

Knowing that you want to target the small firm market
is just the beginning. With so many small firms, how
can you pinpoint the right firms for you? Your first step
is to establish parameters. Identify small firms within
the geographic areas that interest you, as well as
practice areas that inspire you, and try to connect with
law firms that fall within those parameters.

By identifying practice areas and geographic
preferences, you will avoid the "Just Give Me a Job
Syndrome" that plagues so many law students. You
will feel more in control of the job search process and
interview more effectively if you can identify some
geographic and practice area guidelines for your
search. When considering geography, think about
the following factors:

✓ **Where you attended law school.** Law schools, particularly regional law schools, have geographic strongholds where alumni tend to cluster. Since alumni may be favorably disposed to hiring fellow graduates, remaining in the region where you attended law school might inure to your benefit when looking for employment. Use commonsense when choosing a location and consider how competitive a particular legal market may be based on the number of lawyers in practice. For example, while Madison, Wisconsin, is a great place to live and attend law school, it is a highly competitive market, and you will encounter stiff competition for entry-level jobs.

✓ **Where you attended college.** A similar theory applies to college affiliation. If you are going to use your college connections to find employment, it might be helpful to figure out where significant numbers of your fellow alumni live and work. Use your undergraduate career center and alumni office for assistance.

✓ **Where you grew up.** Assess the area where you were raised and look at employment options there. Particularly in small towns or rural regions, having a hometown connection will be a strong plus when seeking employment.

✓ **Where the legal market is thriving.** You are bound to find more job opportunities generally in a strong legal market. Since law is a service industry, it stands to reason that regions experiencing population growth will experience a growing need for legal services. Follow the news and become an expert in the regional legal markets.

✓ **Where your chosen practice area is flourishing.** Certain practice niches flourish in particular geographic locales. If you decide that you simply must practice admiralty law, don't set your sights on Omaha. Better to look at cities like Boston or Philadelphia where admiralty law enjoys a stronghold. Similarly, if you want to practice solely in the area of mergers and acquisitions, avoid small rural counties where the likelihood of finding a steady diet of work in that type of practice is nil. The more you know and understand about the legal market, the better choices you will make in your job search.

You do not necessarily need to make a practice area decision, since many small firms tend to be general practice operations. It might be a good strategy to become a generalist rather than a specialist early in your career with a smaller firm, unless you have a specific area of interest that beckons to you. Electing to pursue specific practice areas can, however, work in your favor if you are looking at boutique firms in areas such as family law or employee benefits law.

Information Gathering

Once you've created some parameters for yourself, the information gathering phase should be easier because you can focus on the important things and avoid wasting time grasping at anything that comes along. To learn about small firms that fall in the geographic area of choice or within the practice areas that interest you, consider the following resources:

- **Career Services Office**

Your law school career services office should have several different resources for you to tap about the small firm market in your area. Some offices maintain directories of local area small firm employers or mentor databases to help connect you to small firm practitioners both locally and nationally. Your school probably sponsors educational programs featuring small firm practitioners. Make an appointment to learn about specific resources in your office. If you are looking in another city or state, consider asking for reciprocity to visit another law school's career services office and use their resources.

- **Faculty**

Professors are an excellent resource for learning about practice options and identifying small firm practitioners. Make it a point to speak with your faculty advisor or any professor with whom you feel a rapport and talk about small firm opportunities. Some faculty serve as of counsel to smaller firms and might have excellent insight into the market. Other faculty may have prior small firm experience and be able to share their knowledge with you.

● **Bar Associations**

National, state, and local bar associations offer a variety of services for small firm practitioners. Tap into these resources to learn about the market and to meet lawyers. Many bar associations offer student memberships that entitle you to attend meetings. In addition, some bar associations offer job placement and job posting services to help connect you to employment opportunities. Find out what your local bar association's membership policies and services are and use these connections to gather information.

● **Publications**

Business and legal publications abound with information about the local economy, movers and shakers within the legal profession, and other interesting tidbits. If you don't already do so, make it a point to begin each day by skimming the local newspaper as well as a national publication such as *The Wall Street Journal* or *The New York Times*. The more sophisticated you become about the business of law and the economy within which it is conducted, the more effective you will be in your job search. Plus, being knowledgeable will make you a more interesting interviewee.

● **The Internet**

A wide range of Internet resources can help you to gather information and learn about career opportunities. See the Appendix beginning on page 150 for a list of Internet sites that might be helpful.

- **Professional Recruiting Agencies**

Professional recruiting agencies, also known as legal search consultants or "headhunters," help to place lawyers in law firm positions and receive fees directly from firms for filling positions. These fees typically range from between 25% to 33% of the starting salary. Most professional recruiting agencies will not handle law student inquiries, although there are exceptions to this rule. Until you pass a state bar examination, you can find placement work as a paralegal. Once you pass a bar examination and have at least one year of experience, many professional legal recruiters will have an interest so long as your credentials match with positions they seek to fill.

Beware of recruiting agencies that ask for fees up front to assist with résumé preparation or to add you to their database. The typical practice for professional legal recruiters is not to receive fees of any sort from the job candidate, but from the firm conducting the hiring instead. If you are concerned about the possibility of an unscrupulous recruiting agency, contact the Better Business Bureau or the Chamber of Commerce in your area. Also consult your career services office to put them on notice.

Networking

Networking is essential to your information gathering process and vital to your ultimate job search success. Employment studies nationwide indicate that between 75% and 85% of all jobs are filled through networking, word-of-mouth contacts, and friendly connections. This is particularly the case with small firms. In the case of large firms, on-campus interviewing is the primary means of filling entry-level vacancies. This is because large firms, like large corporations, can project hiring needs several years in advance. Small firms do not enjoy the luxury of forecasting hiring and growth needs so far in the future. In fact, many small firms depend on word-of-mouth recommendations and other personal contacts when making hiring decisions. So, networking is truly a skill you need to acquire and use when pursuing the small firm market.

Think of networking as a reciprocal arrangement of asking for and offering information instead of as a selfish pursuit of your personal ends. The sooner you reframe your conception of networking from a debasing or embarrassing experience to a positive and career-enhancing process, the better off you will be.

How do you begin to network? First, outline your goals. Simply asking someone for help finding a job is too vague and won't yield the kind of information that you need. So, begin by taking the time to hone your career goals a bit. It's not necessary to focus on a single goal, but try to have some basic themes in mind, such as finding an associate position with a small medical malpractice firm. Decide what you think interests you

➡ Networking Fundamentals

When making hiring decisions, small law firms place a high value on subjective criteria such as personality and communication skills. I think the most effective marketing of law students' skills occurs through networking contacts. If you have personal connections, use them. If not, then learn to cultivate your networking skills. Two strategies that are helpful:

1. Join an organization that interests you. For example, if you are interested in family law or children's issues, look into serving on the Foster Care Review Board or volunteering at Juvenile Court. Join the Junior Chamber of Commerce, or any other organization whose members are likely to include lawyers and business people. Getting to know people in a social or philanthropic setting is much more conducive to relationship-building than a typical mass mailing. People like to help people they know and like. Don't assume that because you are not in a city in which you want to practice that developing contacts isn't important. Lawyers are likely to have lawyer friends in other cities and personal contact can open the doors that letters and résumés cannot.

2. If you know a lawyer who practices nearby, ask her/him if you can "shadow" them at court on motion day. Not only will this provide an opportunity to see what goes on in court, but it may also be an opportunity to meet more lawyers. If you're personable, the lawyers you meet may remember you. And, they might be impressed by your initiative.

Dorris A. Smith
Assistant Director of Career Services
Vanderbilt University Law School

and endeavor to learn more about it. As suggested earlier, creating some geographic parameters will also help you to focus your information gathering process.

- **Making Networking Contacts**

    Here are some ideas for making connections through networking:

    ✓ Share your career goals with others at your law school — professors, staff, and classmates. (If you are a law student, recognize that taking the time now to build relationships with professors, staff, and classmates will provide you with a network you can continue to tap after graduation; if you are a graduate, remember to include law school contacts in your networking.)

    ✓ Attend educational programs organized by your career services office as a means of connecting with lawyers.

    ✓ Tap your local bar association for information about memberships or programs; student memberships are often available.

    Outside law school, talk to everyone — neighbors, friends, former employers, and family members — about your goals. Don't limit your contacts to lawyers.

    Use the Internet to connect with small firms. Sites specializing in legal jobs abound. (See the Appendix beginning on page 150 for a list of helpful Internet sites.)

Investigate whether your undergraduate college offers any Internet-based networking services to reach fellow alumni. Searches using the Martindale-Hubbell database will yield college or law school graduates who might be willing to speak with you. Some sample searches using the Martindale-Hubbell database on LexisNexis® can be found in the Appendix on page 154.

● **Making the Approach**

Approaching someone for assistance is probably the most difficult part of the networking process for most of us. Contact anxiety stems from several factors, including shyness, fear of rejection, embarrassment from having to ask for help in the first place, and a feeling that you are imposing on others. Approach networking connections by telephone, by letter or e-mail, or in person. You should choose the method that suits you the best. Letter or e-mail is probably the most convenient mode because it allows the recipient to choose the time of reply and avoids the possibility of interrupting someone at an inconvenient time. This is particularly true with small firms, where time constraints are acute.

Keep your correspondence concise and direct. Introduce yourself and state your connection immediately. Describe your interests and offer the recipient the chance to contact you. Avoid enclosing a résumé or any other materials that might smack of asking for a job in your initial contact. For example:

Dean Daniel Brown suggested that I contact you regarding my interest in environmental law. After

I shared my enthusiasm for pursuing a career as an environmental lawyer, Dean Brown thought you would be able to offer some advice about how to proceed with my career. Last summer, I clerked for the Department of Environmental Protection and realized that this practice area was especially meaningful to me.

I realize that you are busy but would appreciate the chance to speak with you briefly in person or by telephone to learn more about your practice. I can be reached at _____ or via e-mail at _____. Thank you in advance for your time and assistance. I look forward to speaking with you about your work.

You can also telephone potential networking contacts, although a telephone call out of the blue might not be the wisest first contact for busy lawyers. If you do decide to call, be direct in telephone calls. Begin by stating, "Professor Jane Rose, who taught my first-year Contracts class, suggested that I give you a call. Is this a good time to talk?" If you reach someone's voice mail, leave a brief message and be sure to give clear directions for reaching you.

When you meet with a networking contact, come prepared with an agenda. First and foremost, you are gathering information from an expert source. Consider asking questions such as:

✓ What made you decide to practice in a small firm environment?

✓ What aspect of your work do you enjoy the most?

✓ What kinds of skills do you think small firm practitioners should cultivate?

✓ What advice do you have about courses I should take next semester?

✓ What kinds of job prospects exist with small firms in this geographic market?

✓ How can I distinguish myself with a small firm in this job market?

Listen carefully to what is being said. Remember to converse, not interrogate. Your goal is to leave a networking meeting with a better understanding of what you want to do and how to achieve your goals. If a networking contact offers names of others to speak with, ask permission to use the contact's name in subsequent correspondence.

After meeting with a contact, be sure to write a thank you letter promptly. Convey your thanks and, if other contacts were suggested, remind the reader that you will be following up. For example:

> *Thank you again for taking the time to share your experiences as a litigator in a small firm. I appreciate your candor and admire the enthusiasm you have for your work. Per your suggestion, I will register for the Legal Services Clinic in order to gain more experience in court with clients. I hope this will improve my marketability with smaller firms in the area. I will keep you apprised of my progress and appreciate all your help.*

Networking is, in essence, give-and-take, not take-and-take as some believe it to be. It is an opportunity to share information, learn from an expert, and develop further contacts. Compared to the sterile process of responding to a job posting, networking is full of serendipitous potential, particularly for a person interested in being hired by a small firm where predictable hiring schedules are not the norm.

The Importance of Networking

Although networking is not the only method of finding a job, when you are dealing with small firms, it is the best way! Small firms have neither the staff nor the budget to carry on a major recruitment campaign. Word of mouth is how most positions at small firms are filled. One of the easiest but often overlooked methods of networking is just talking to people and letting them know that you are looking for a job. The more people who know you are looking, the more likely your name is to be passed on to the right person.

As a counselor, I have had many occasions to see students visibly cringe when I mention the word "networking." It is almost as if I suggested they try jumping out of a plane without a parachute. The first thing students usually say is "I don't know any lawyers." That is okay; you do not have to know a lawyer, you just have to know someone who knows a lawyer. Think of all the people you know and then think of all the people they know or come in contact with. Your neighbor, your college roommate, your professors, members of your running club, your old boss, etc. They may have a spouse who is an attorney, a parent or sibling, or they may have attorneys they work with or clients they deal with who are lawyers.

Since you never know who might be helpful in putting you in contact with a prospective employer, it is best to tell as many people as possible about your situation. Here are three real-life success stories:

1. One Carolina student went home for winter break. In church on Sunday, he sat next to an elderly woman whom he had not seen in five years. When she asked him what he was doing, among other things he mentioned he was a first-year law student and was trying to decide what kind of legal job he would pursue for the upcoming summer.

When the service was over, he noticed the woman "dragging" a gentleman across the church to where he was standing. The man turned out to be a senior partner at a local firm. They established a relationship, the student kept in touch and was offered a job for that summer.

2. Another student used her spring break to volunteer in Miami to help recent immigrants with legal matters. There were other volunteers, including a sole practitioner specializing in immigration law who had never hired a summer clerk before. By the end of the week they had gotten to know each other, the attorney had an opportunity to see the student's work, and she was asked to clerk the next summer.

3. Another student was stressing about not yet having a job for the summer. She decided to go horseback riding to clear her mind. When she got to the stables, the groom started talking to her and she blurted out her worries. He didn't say much, just listened. His next client was the spouse of an attorney. He told the client about the law student's concerns and what a great person she was. To make a long story short, she had a meeting with the attorney. The student was hired for the summer and ended up working for this firm when she graduated.

Ellen Stark Hill
Assistant Director, Career Services Office
UNC School of Law, Chapel Hill, NC

NETWORKING DOS and DON'TS

Before approaching a networking prospect:

- Consider networking as a process to gather information. Never ask for a job.

- Begin your correspondence with the connection you want to highlight.

- Whether you correspond by regular mail or e-mail, make sure your introductory message is concise and free of typographical errors.

- Have a résumé available, but don't furnish it with your initial correspondence/contact.

When you meet your networking prospect:

- Set the agenda and come prepared with questions; don't ambush your networking contact by turning the meeting into an interview.

- Inquire about the dress code for the office and dress appropriately.

- Remain friendly, but not familiar. Do not feel that you are entitled to anything other than an information gathering meeting.

After meeting your networking prospect:

- Be prompt with your thank you letter and follow up with all subsequent contacts your networking prospect suggests. Your networking web will begin to expand quickly if you follow up on all leads.

- Keep your networking contact apprised of your progress. Holiday cards or other informal correspondence are perfectly appropriate ways to remain in your contact's thoughts. One good strategy is to clip relevant articles to send to contacts with a thoughtful note.

- Help others in need in the future. Think of networking as a give-and-take rather than a winner-take-all experience. Consider it a privilege to help another person achieve his or her dreams.

➡ The Internet as a Networking Resource

Networking has always been a great way to learn about careers and employers and to find and land the right job. However, the Internet has dramatically expanded an individual's ability to connect and communicate with people who can be helpful to one's job search. For example, there are fantastic discussions taking place on WetFeet.com's discussion boards about everything from what it's like to be an African-American in a corporate environment, to what it's like to be a lawyer in a startup. Not only would it be hard to connect with so many people who can share information about these topics, it would be impossible to sustain such a rich discussion without the capabilities and access provided by the Internet.

Steve Pollock
President and Co-Founder
WetFeet.com

Part-time or Contract Work as an Entry Point

If you are a second- or third-year student, consider offering to work on a part-time basis during the school year as a means of getting your foot in the door with a small firm. In addition to earning some extra money, working part-time offers you the chance to develop some real-world lawyering skills that you can add to your résumé.

Since most small firms are not in a position to run extensive summer associate programs, the best way lawyers can test-drive possible full-time hires is to get to know them and the quality of their work. For this reason, part-time employment during the academic year or contract work following graduation can be a natural segue into a full-time position with a small firm. Should a full-time opening occur, you are in the unique position of being an instantly credible candidate, since the firm will know the quality of your work product as well as your character and work ethic.

Part-time employment also provides you with the opportunity to develop a mentor relationship with an experienced attorney, to learn the business of law, and to hone your practice skills. Beyond the mentoring possibilities, part-time work is an introduction into a larger world of networking. Knowing a lawyer and having the lawyer know the quality of your work will enable you to meet other lawyers in the community and extend your circle of professional acquaintances. Finding full-time employment is part *what* you know and part *who* you know.

If you decide to pursue part-time employment as a means of securing full-time work with a small firm, keep in mind that you cannot depend on representations made by a smaller employer about their long-term personnel needs because a small firm's needs can change very quickly. While this should not be construed to mean that you should jump from part-time job to part-time job in relentless pursuit of a possible full-time offer, you should keep your eyes and ears open at the office and know what is going on to the extent you are able. For example, if you are working for two partners and learn that the child of one of the partners is graduating from law school this year and wants to join the practice, you need to assess the probability of being hired on a full-time basis. Similarly, if you perceive that business is very slow, think about how this will play out in the coming months when you need a full-time position. The final word: don't rely on any promises, and always keep your options open while maintaining your professionalism.

● Finding Part-time Employment

If you decide that working part-time will help you find the small firm job you want on a full-time basis, the best place to start is your career services office. Typically, openings for part-time jobs are posted for all to see. Your school might also post part-time jobs on its website, on the law school e-mail distribution list, or via a newsletter.

Be prepared to fax or send a cover letter and résumé to employers. Time is of the essence in small firm hiring, so be on the look-out for postings and respond immediately. Submitting materials by fax is perfectly acceptable since the quicker you are to apply, the sooner the small firm employer can fill the position. Unlike large firms with attenuated hiring processes, small firms have more immediate needs and appreciate a quick response.

You can also initiate your own part-time job search by seeking out small firms that practice in your areas of interest. Consult online resources such as the LexisNexis® Martindale-Hubbell database. If your local bar association offers a membership directory, use it to find local small firm practitioners in particular practice areas by referring to specific section or division listings.

- ● **Contract/Temporary Attorney Opportunities**

If you want to tap into the small firm market after completing law school, you might consider working as a contract or temporary attorney in order to gain experience and foster connections. Contract attorneys are hired through agencies to work on discrete issues. Temporary attorneys, as the name implies, work on a temporary basis to fill in for full-time attorneys on leave or when work suddenly outstrips capacity. Temporary attorneys may be individual freelance attorneys but today they are more frequently contracted through an agency. The terms *contract attorney* and *temporary attorney* have thus become almost indistinguishable.

Some graduates choose to become contract attorneys because they are seeking flexibility in their work schedules or are looking for full-time work but need to earn money while they are searching. Contract work is a great way to gain experience in a particular practice

➡️ Transitioning from Contract Attorney Work to Permanent Law Firm Employment

Contract work provides many valuable benefits, including hands-on experience, flexibility, variety, and a steady paycheck to bridge the gap in difficult times. But if you decide to transition from contract work to permanent law firm employment, you will face a unique challenge that you may find surprising.

The source of this unique challenge is this: because law firms endeavor to project an image of strength and stability to their clients and the general public, they actively seek to hire attorneys who appear to possess those attributes. Unfortunately, many firms equate contract work with weakness and/or instability, and therefore tend to look down on contract work when hiring permanent attorneys. Firms often perceive that contract attorneys are less committed to the practice of law than those who have permanent positions and/or that they lack the skills and credentials necessary to succeed in a permanent position. Their impression is that someone who works as a contract attorney does so only because he or she is unwilling or unable to work in a permanent position. Therefore, in many instances, a firm would rather fill a permanent position by hiring an attorney who is currently unemployed but previously worked in a permanent position with a prestigious firm than a currently employed contract attorney.

Clearly, these perceptions of contract attorneys are unfair or inaccurate in many instances. But they exist nevertheless. Therefore, to maximize your chances of success in your job search, you should address them in your initial contact with firms. (As a general rule, these perceptions are most prevalent among prestigious large law firms. Generally it is not quite as difficult to transition from contract work to permanent employment with a smaller firm. But you should cast your contract work in the best possible light no matter what the size of your target firm. This is especially true because small firms tend to be conservative in their hiring; their size requires that they hire candidates who are likely to stay with the firm for the long term.)

If you are represented by a reputable legal recruiter, the recruiter can ease the way for you in this regard, advocating on your behalf, optimizing your résumé, and explaining your situation to hiring coordinators. If you are approaching firms on your own, however, you must address these perceptions in your résumé and cover letter. Following are some suggestions for crafting a résumé and cover letter that counter these negative preconceptions and present your contract work as a strength that will add value to the firm.

First, make sure that your résumé effectively describes the nature and complexity of the contract work you performed. If the work you handled was challenging and interesting, make sure that your résumé reflects this. Additionally, if the firm has given you increasing amounts of responsibility or progressively more sophisticated work during your tenure as a contract attorney, that should be apparent from your résumé as well; anything that tends to demonstrate strong, consistent performance should be included.

Second, prepare a brief, articulate cover letter in which you explain why you accepted work as a contract attorney and why you are now seeking to transition to permanent employment. Attorneys have various reasons for doing contract work, some of which are quite understandable to firms (e.g., relocating to a new state where passage of the bar examination is a prerequisite to recommencing practice; needing flexibility to care for a seriously ill relative who has since recovered; desiring exposure to a new practice area). If you explain at the outset your reasons for accepting contract work — in a succinct and non-defensive manner — the hiring coordinator is more likely to look favorably upon your candidacy. Moreover, if you accepted contract work due to a situation or set of circumstances that has resolved, your desire to transition to permanent employment will make business sense to the reader.

Finally, use your cover letter to build upon the description of your contract work contained in your résumé. Do not simply repeat what is written on your résumé, but rather explain why your contract work is relevant to the position for which you are applying and how it will enable you to add value to the firm's practice. While you should never overstate your skills or exaggerate your knowledge of a firm, you should demonstrate that you are aware of the firm's core practice areas and strengths, have a genuine interest in practicing there, and have transferable skills that will allow you to excel.

Keep in mind that you need to make a business case for why it makes sense for the firm to hire you. Try to step back from your own situation and evaluate your candidacy from the point of view of the law firm's hiring coordinator (who often is deluged with résumés, has limited time, and is under pressure to satisfy the hiring needs of demanding partners). Doing so will enable you to craft a résumé and cover letter that are not only accurate but persuasive, engaging, and instrumental in helping you secure an outstanding new position.

Jennifer McKee
BCG Attorney Search

area. Litigation is particularly well-suited to contract work since it can be divided into discrete projects such as document review or research and brief writing on specific topics. While statistics are not generally available, anecdotal evidence suggests that contract work is a means to securing full-time work because it familiarizes an employer with the quality of a lawyer's skills.

Your law school's career services office should have the names of local, regional, and national contract attorney agencies. Compensation will vary depending upon the market, the law firm seeking to hire you, and your level of experience. Until you successfully pass the bar, you will probably be considered either a paralegal or law clerk and paid accordingly.

Lateral Hiring

Lateral hiring refers to hiring a candidate who has graduated from law school, passed the bar examination, and has prior legal work experience. Lateral hiring is on the rise and is likely to continue to increase according to national studies. Changing jobs is a common feature of legal practice today. *Keeping the Keepers II: Mobility and Management of Associates*, a 2003 study by The NALP Foundation, found that the average annual attrition rate for entry-level associates was 13.8%. Within the first two years of practice, nearly 25% of the associates at law firms of all sizes move on. According to the study, after nearly five years, more than half of those hired out of law school have left their original firms. In short, lawyers can expect to change employers several times during the course of their careers.

Once you have some post-graduate legal experience, moving to a smaller firm becomes a bit easier since you bring with you some real-world skills and, perhaps, some clients. Since smaller firms are less able to spend time training new attorneys, having some experience will be viewed favorably by employers.

If you are looking for small firm opportunities after working for several years, you should consider making direct contact, using resources through your local bar association and career services office, and using a professional recruiter (legal search consultant). Because search consultants receive fees from employers with whom they place an attorney and because those fees can amount to as much as one-third of the attorney's salary, hiring through a search consultant is expensive for the employer. Smaller employers may be more likely to question this expense and may, in addition, hire too infrequently to have established close working relationships with search consultants. For these reasons, consider initiating an independent job search before turning to a professional recruiter.

The Paper Chase: Résumés, Cover Letters, and Writing Samples

Once you have determined your parameters, gathered information, and started the networking process, it's time to contact law firms and express your interest. Whether responding to a specific posting or creating a tailored mailing to particular firms, you need to present your "paper self" effectively in order to reach the next step, securing an interview. This section will discuss the creation of outstanding résumés, cover letters, and writing samples that will distinguish you from the pack.

- **Résumés**

Your résumé is the document that memorializes your relevant qualifications for the job you are seeking. The key word here is "relevant." Don't be misled into believing that creating a multi-page résumé detailing all of your student leadership experiences and every job you ever held will be relevant to a small firm. An endless list of minimum wage jobs, undergraduate clubs, and sorority accomplishments takes a long time to read and forces the employer to work too hard in an attempt to discern what distinguishes you from the other candidates. Simplify the employer's life by focusing them on the qualifications that truly matter.

For example, if you are applying to a firm that specializes in family law, be sure to list all relevant family law courses, details of past jobs that included family law issues, any volunteer experience that included family law, and the like. By focusing the

➡️ ## Résumés — What One Firm Values

We are a 12-person firm in Salt Lake City, Utah, with a "big firm" practice in complex commercial and employment litigation. Describing what we value in a résumé is simple. We value the substance of the résumé. Economically and philosophically, we do not hire a new lawyer merely because he or she meets our hiring criteria and we hope the relationship will work. We hire only those lawyers whose qualities and potential are exciting to us. Describing how a résumé reveals these qualities and otherwise distinguishes a candidate is complex.

First, don't distinguish yourself in the wrong ways. Include all the basic information — law school performance, educational history, work history, volunteer and community work, awards, personal interests, and the like. Don't be careless. Typos in a résumé or cover letter demonstrate that a candidate doesn't meet our work quality expectations. The longer your cover letter, the more likely it is to have typos.

Find out who we are. Read our NALP materials, look at our Martindale–Hubbell listing and visit our website. Ask other attorneys about our firm, our reputation, and our philosophy. When you submit a résumé to a small firm, it will likely be reviewed by at least one of the firm's founders. That person had, and still has, a significant role in shaping the firm's philosophy and the quality of work it expects from its attorneys. When we review a résumé, we look for signs of a talented lawyer who will be as passionate about our firm's philosophy and standards as we are. Make sure your résumé or cover letter demonstrates your familiarity with our lawyers, practice areas, philosophy, and expectations.

Let us know who you are. While we look for academic achievement and a strong work ethic, that isn't enough. Our lawyers have a broad diversity of interests, experience, backgrounds, and personalities. We are citizens of our community and want to associate with people who have interests and abilities outside the profession. As a small firm, this diversity is crucial to maintaining a dynamic practice and working environment. We want to know how you can contribute to it. Include descriptions of your community involvement and personal interests on your résumé.

Mary C. Gordon, Hiring Partner
Manning Curtis Bradshaw & Bednar LLC
Salt Lake City, Utah

IN THEIR OWN WORDS . . .

➡ The Unerasable Résumé Glitch

In the last decade, we've all become accustomed to taking advantage of the World Wide Web — for job searching, legal research, general information, and just plain goofing off. However, unlike many forms of communication, your online voice can come back and haunt you in the employment world years down the road.

Prospective employers are doing more in-depth background checks today, made easier by the simple "Googling" of a prospect's name. If you do not already do so, try it yourself. You may find a silly comment made on a political or entertainment site that has nothing to do with lawyering or the legal profession — but might reflect poorly to the conservative law firm set.

As you probably know, the larger the law firm or corporation, the less likely that you're free-spirited, First Amendment voice will be seen as a plus. If a firm has the equivalent of "corporate communications," you may be officially or unofficially forbidden from voicing what might be considered a reflection of the law firm. The good news for those seeking employment in the small- to mid-size law firm market is that independence and creativity are generally more widely accepted.

While web logs or "blogs" can be an excellent résumé enhancer (in showing legal expertise in a particular practice niche), they can also be deadly in the job hunt. If you think about how painstakingly you prep for job interview Q&As, think about how an employer might react (or wince) at what you've posted for the whole wide world to see. Many of the most successful lawyer bloggers are independent in the workplace as well as on the web — for a reason.

Keep the following in mind:

- Just because you delete a web page or posting does not mean it is no longer accessible. The "cached" page could still be found on a web search and be read and printed.

- Even though online bulletin boards, listservs, and blogs might seem private or closed, you really have no idea about the readership. Assume everyone from your boss to grandmother could read it.

- "Cut and paste" and "forward" (or, even worse, "forward to all") should be kept in mind when saying something on a web site, blog, or in an e-mail.

Since 1997, when I became known in the legal industry as the "Internet Marketing Attorney," I have seen instances of people losing their jobs (and opportunities) because of postings read by employers. Young associates have lost jobs by showing youth in comments made online that have quickly found their way back to employers (including embarrassing press coverage of the ill-advised blunders). I have first-hand experience having lost a job because the employer simply did not understand the web (even though they were in the legal publishing business). I know of another attorney who had an employer that did not like her freewheeling blog (again, it had nothing to do with her job or profession). A few have shot themselves in the foot with online postings that were all too easy to identify.

If your goal is to use a web site or blog to enhance your marketability, treat it like a résumé. Just remember, you might not be able to change it later!

Micah Buchdahl
President
HTMLawyers, Inc.

employer's attention on the things that matter most to his or her practice, you signal your interest in the firm and help connect your qualifications to the needs of the employer.

Studies indicate that employers typically spend *30 seconds* reviewing a résumé. Make every second count by keeping your résumé compact, easy to read and simple to follow up on. Here are some tips to create an aesthetically pleasing résumé:

✓ **Limit your résumé to one page.** Since employers will scan a résumé for less than a minute, lengthy résumés will not be read in their entirety. In fact, if the important information is not readily available on the first page, it's unlikely the employer will read further. As a general rule, consider one page for every ten years' of experience. This rule might vary from person to person, but it's a good guideline. Should you feel compelled to move to a multi-page résumé, put the most important information on the first page. That way, your salient qualifications will be readily available in case the employer has no time to read further.

✓ **Use a legible font size.** Some people try to get around the aforementioned "one page" rule by presenting the information in small 8-point type. This is much too small for the average person to read comfortably. Don't remind the employer that he or she needs bifocals. Use 10-point or 12-point font size and make sure your font size remains consistent throughout your résumé. It's very disconcerting to read a résumé that moves between three font sizes and multiple typefaces. Also, if you know a potential employer uses a scanning program to input data into a searchable database, the differing font sizes will render your résumé unscannable.

✓ **Choose typefaces that are clear and easy to read.** Consider fonts such as Times New Roman or Arial. Stay consistent with your typeface. It's confusing to the eye to read multiple typefaces, particularly script or gothic typefaces.

✓ **Select a neutral paper color.** White, ivory (or cream or buff), and gray are ideal. Make sure the paper reproduces well and doesn't become difficult to read when later photocopied. Some students feel that livening up their résumés with punchy colors will call attention to their credentials, and choose purples, pinks, colorful borders, or bold graphics. Avoid the temptation to be outrageous. You might get some short-lived attention, but it may not be the kind of attention you seek to attract.

✓ **Use good quality bond paper for your résumé and cover letter.** Don't buy expensive brands with fancy watermarks. Any good office supply store will have résumé quality paper that you can buy in bulk. Assume you'll need at least 200 envelopes and 400 pieces of bond paper for résumés, cover letters, and thank you and follow-up correspondence.

✓ **Use matching envelopes.** Your cover letter and your envelope should match. Buy in bulk at an office supply store, and you'll have plenty of matching stationery to get you through your job search.

● **What Small Firms Value — What to Emphasize on Your Résumé**

Small firms care about many of the same things that any size legal employer cares about: they want to hire qualified individuals who will do the job well and enjoy their work enough to contribute to the success of the business. Smaller firms, however, might emphasize different skills and qualities in making their hiring decisions.

For example, grades matter less to smaller firms than evidence of substantive skills. A small civil litigation firm will be more inclined to overlook the "C+" you received in Criminal Law and value the "A" you garnered in Legal Research & Analysis. Clinical experience will often be viewed favorably, since it indicates an ability to handle a case from client counseling to research and resolution of the issue. Prior legal experience, such as summer jobs and part-time work during the school year, will likely be valued, because it demonstrates practical lawyering skills and an understanding of the business of law.

Small firms value hard workers, so showcase evidence of your work ethic. Consider how you might frame your work experience in terms that convey that you are a hard worker. Perhaps, for example, some of your jobs during law school do not seem relevant, but collectively they demonstrate how you worked your way through law school; let employers know about that accomplishment, particularly if you do not have much other work experience to showcase.

For sample résumés, see the Appendix beginning on page 169.

Cover Letters: The 1-2-3 Model for Success

Think of your cover letter as the very first writing sample a potential employer reads. Many students are convinced that employers disregard cover letters and review résumés only. Wrong! Cover letters are scrutinized carefully for content and style, and most especially for accuracy. A well-written cover letter can make the difference between an interview and the circular file, so think about what you want to say and how you're going to say it.

Consider my 1-2-3 model for cover letters and use it as a guide for your own correspondence. Ideally, cover letters should be three paragraphs long. Each paragraph should contain at least three sentences, and each statement should be backed up with no more than three examples of your skills. Anything longer than three paragraphs or any description that exceeds three sentences risks dragging the reader down with needless detail. You need to make your points clearly and concisely and let your résumé describe your relevant accomplishments more fully. Here is an outline of the ideal 1-2-3 cover letter:

● **The Model 1-2-3 Cover Letter**

✓ **Paragraph 1: Introduce Yourself.** Describe who you are, your connection (if any) to the reader, and the job for which you would like to be considered.

✓ **Paragraph 2: Connect Your Relevant Skills to the Job.** This is your chance to describe relevant work or academic experiences which would bear on the job for which you are applying. Give examples to back up your claims. Describe substantive work experiences, particularly in-depth research and writing projects. When you contact an employer, make some effort to match your skills with the firm's practice. This does not require lots of time and effort. You simply need to do a bit of research beforehand. For example, if the firm practices insurance defense litigation, you need to know something about insurance defense practice and you need to enunciate why you are interested in that kind of law. It's a complete waste of time to write bland cover letters or, worse, cover letters that miss the mark completely. You'll never get an interview with an intellectual property firm if you express an interest in plaintiff's personal injury work in your cover letter.

✓ **Paragraph 3: Thanks, Please Call.** Thank the reader and provide accurate information about where you can be reached, both by telephone and e-mail. Be sure, by the way, to have a reliable answering machine with an appropriately professional message. Check both your voice mail and e-mail regularly — a timely response demonstrates your interest in the job and your reliability.

COVER LETTER DOS AND DON'TS

- **Cover letters must be free of typographical errors and grammatically correct.** Spell-checking on your computer is fine, but you also need to proof your cover letter carefully to avoid any errors. Have someone read your cover letter for logic and flow. Your law school career services office is a great place to get feedback and suggestions. You would be surprised at the frequency with which hiring attorneys throw away materials from candidates who misspell their firm's name or, worse yet, the addressee's name.

- **"To Whom It May Concern" should never be your salutation.** You need to write to a living, breathing human being, preferably the lawyer in charge of hiring. When you address a letter "To Whom It May Concern," you send a message that you do not care enough to learn the name of the decision-maker.

- **Cover letters must be typed.** Never hand write a cover letter!

Contacting Small Firms

In my experience, mass mailings do not work well for small firms. Networking is very important through resources like the small firm section of your local bar association, as would be responding to ads. Consider placing an ad in your local bar journal to contact potential employers.

> Donald E. Teller, Jr.
> Law Office of Donald E. Teller, Jr., P.C.
> Colleyville, Texas

For examples of cover letters and other related correspondence, see the Appendix beginning on page 162. Other resources pertaining to business correspondence can be found in the Appendix on page 151.

You do not have to write a different cover letter for every single employer you contact. Creating a template that you can tailor based on the 1-2-3 model will ease your cover letter writing duties immeasurably. Once you have the basic model complete, outlining your relevant skills, you can customize as the need arises.

● **Conduct Follow Up: Make a Phone Call!**

Follow-up to your cover letter is absolutely essential, especially with small firms. It is a common mistake on the part of students to believe that simply mailing a cover letter and résumé completes the application process. I frequently speak to law students who send several dozen cover letters to employers and then wait — and wait — and wait some more, sometimes for months on end. Unless an employer specifies "no phone calls," you should either e-mail or telephone between five and ten business days after your mailing to follow up. What do you say? Here are some suggestions:

✓ *Hello, this is Donna Gerson. I sent you a cover letter and résumé regarding the position you posted at the University of Pittsburgh. I just wanted to tell you how interested I am in the position and that I would be able to interview this Friday since I don't have any classes scheduled.*

✓ *Good morning. My name is Donna Gerson and I was calling because I sent a cover letter and résumé to inquire about any part-time law clerk jobs you might have. Is this a good time to call?*

A small firm hiring partner inundated with work might appreciate the initiative and may be inclined to schedule an interview simply because you took the time to call.

Writing Samples

Writing samples offer employers the opportunity to see your writing style and analytical skill. Typically, writing samples are not sent with résumés and cover letters. However, it is a good practice to bring a writing sample to an interview and offer it for review.

WRITING SAMPLE DOS AND DON'TS

- **Keep the length of your writing sample between five and eight pages.** If you have a longer piece, consider taking one section and using that as your writing sample.

- **Use your best work, regardless of the topic.** Ideally, it's great to have your writing sample match the practice area of the employer, but the most important aspect of the writing sample is that it demonstrates your drafting ability.

- **Present neat, cleanly typed samples, but writing samples can be on regular paper instead of expensive bond paper.** It is not necessary to go to that expense.

- **Make sure your former employer knows you are using work you created during your prior employment as a writing sample.** Don't make a gaffe by presenting work that is not expressly permitted to be disseminated to others. If you are told a piece should not be disseminated, ask whether changing the names would make it acceptable as a writing sample.

References

Be prepared with a list of references to offer a prospective employer at an interview. Since an employer is more likely to telephone a reference, all you need to supply is a list containing names, work affiliations, and telephone numbers. Addresses are unnecessary. When considering references, avoid asking friends or family to serve as references. Your goal is to have individuals who know your intellect, your work ethic, and your substantive research and writing skills.

With that in mind, you should think about professors and former legal employers. With professors, it's better to approach those who taught you in smaller classes and who actually know your skills rather than someone who taught a large section and only got to know you through the Socratic method. "Big Name" references will fall flat if those individuals cannot speak about you in a genuine way.

Communications in the Information Age

A growing number of small firms use the Internet for business development and correspondence. Depending on the breadth and quality of the firm's website content, visitors can learn biographical information about the firm's lawyers, contact information, and representative cases and clients, and gain access to articles by the firm's attorneys.

Use e-mail to make networking contacts and to apply for positions, particularly when e-mail reply is specified. Employers who use e-mail recognize that it's convenient, easy to forward to colleagues, and easy to reply to. Since the essence of e-mail communication is its instantaneous nature, you need to check your e-mail often and reply promptly. Some sample e-mail correspondence follows in the Appendix section beginning on page 150.

Answering machines and voice mail are essential to your job search, so keep your messages professional and clear. Do not play background music on your message or use gimmicky messages. When leaving a voice mail message for another, be direct and articulate. Always leave your phone number and name clearly and the reason for your message.

If you maintain a personal Web page or blog, make sure it is professional and does not contain any inappropriate information. It's fine to post your résumé online with links to other points of relevant interest. I would advise against using photographs or supplying commentary on anything other than your professional credentials. I have read student websites with lists containing "The Ten Best Places to Party," and other irrelevant information that will only cast doubt on your commonsense and good taste.

➡ Focus on the Small Firm Market in Boston

Boston is a very popular destination for new lawyers. The seven accredited law schools in Massachusetts graduate over 2,000 new lawyers each year. And, 1,832 applicants sat for the July 2004 bar examination, of which 1,591 were first-time takers.

Martindale-Hubbell® (*www.martindale.com*) lists nearly 700 small and medium sized Boston law firms, the majority of which have 1-10 attorneys: 572 firms with 1-10 attorneys; 62 firms with 11-25 attorneys; and 38 firms with 26-50 attorneys.

As in other legal communities, the small firms in Boston hire on an unpredictable "as needed" basis. Although a few small firms consistently hire third-year law students in the fall preceding graduation, most will hire new attorneys at any time during the late spring, summer, or during the fall after the bar examination.

Salaries

The starting salaries for new associates in small firms in the Boston area generally range from $30,000 to $70,000. The median salary for a new associate in Massachusetts in a firm of 2-10 lawyers is $40,000. And, the median salary within a firm of 11-25 lawyers is $52,500 (*Jobs & J.D.'s: Employment and Salaries of New Law Graduates, Class of 2003, NALP*). Although there are some firms that pay considerably more than the median, those firms are typically local branches of large national firms.

Bar Associations and Groups

All of the local bar associations and groups offer wonderful networking opportunities. Three of the local groups are particularly noteworthy:

Boston Bar Association: The BBA (*www.bostonbar.org*) has 20 different sections and countless subsections that meet on a regular basis. In the fall of 2004, the President of the BBA implemented a new initiative to get students more involved with the BBA and the work of the subcommittees. Students are warmly welcomed, and local schools have been invited to send student representatives to each of the sections. A student membership costs $25 and entitles a student to join the New Lawyer's Section.

The Women's Bar Association: The WBA (found on the web at *www.womensbar. org*) has started a new program called Mentoring Circles, comprised of experienced attorneys, newer attorneys, non-practicing attorneys, law students, and members of the judiciary. The WBA also has a Law Student Committee. A student membership costs $25.

The Boston Lawyer's Group: The BLG (found on the web at *www.bostonlawyersgroup.org*) maintains a welcoming presence for students and lawyers of color. The BLG employer members are primarily large law firms with some local government agencies, but the BLG offers helpful programs for all students. In addition to the fall job fair, which caters to the large law firms, the BLG offers a mock interview program, career panels, and a mentoring program.

Local Secret

Anyone who wants to practice law in Boston should subscribe to the local legal community newspaper, *Massachusetts Lawyers Weekly* (*www.masslawyersweekly.com*). The newspaper, which is published every Monday, provides information on the local legal scene. And, the back pages of *Mass Lawyers Weekly* are dedicated to job postings. The job postings are also available online at *www.lawyersweeklyjobs.com* (search "Attorney Positions" in "Massachusetts").

Maris Abbene
Director, Career Services
Boston College Law School

➡ ## Focus on Washington, D.C. Small Firms

It sometimes seems that every other person in Washington, D.C. is a lawyer. Being the nation's capital, D.C. has more than its fair share of very large prestigious law firms, as well as branch offices for almost every leading national law firm. In addition, there is the cadre of attorneys who work for the federal government in both legal and non-legal capacities. Finally, there are the lawyers who work in the large variety of small- and medium-sized firms in and around the city. Although D.C. is not even among the 20 most populous cities in the United States (when excluding its Virginia and Maryland suburbs), it is ranked second in terms of the number of legal jobs it provides to law graduates according to NALP statistics (*Jobs & J.D.'s: Employment and Salaries of New Law Graduates, Class of 2003*).

The small- and medium-sized firm market in D.C. shares many similarities with the small firm market in other urban areas but also has some unique characteristics. As in other cities, attorneys in smaller firms in the D.C. area often serve individual clients and therefore practice in areas such as family law, divorce law, trusts and estates, criminal defense, personal injury, and employment law. In addition to these typical small firm practices, D.C. also has a substantial number of "boutique" law firms with specialties unique to Washington, D.C. Such practices include legislative affairs and lobbying, international law, international trade, associations, nonprofits, energy, FDA, customs, government contracts, and Native American law, to name a few. While large law firms also feature such practices, they by no means have a monopoly, and smaller firms can often be just as effective advocates with equally sophisticated clients in these areas.

For law students and new graduates, it can be a daunting task to identify these boutique law firms and effectively market their skills to those firms. The most comprehensive and useful resource for identifying firms is the *Legal Times Directory of Metro D.C. Law Offices.* This directory lists all firms — large and small — alphabetically within D.C., suburban Maryland, and Northern Virginia, and includes an extensive index which sorts the firms by practice area. Students can also identify firms using Martindale (*www.martindale.com* or on LexisNexis®) and the West Legal Directory found on Westlaw®. I advise students to pick two or three practice areas in which they have a demonstrated interest, background, or experience, and write targeted cover letters to those firms with those practices.

Like most small firms, boutique firms in D.C. hire when they have a need and do not follow any specific hiring season. Because of their narrow focus, these firms are usually more interested in students or graduates who demonstrate an interest in — or have a background related to — the firm's legal specialty, and are less interested in grade point averages. For students who are studying in Washington, D.C., there are many opportunities to gain experience in particular fields through interning with federal agencies during the school year. Students from schools outside D.C. can pursue these opportunities over the summer.

I encourage students to explore options at agencies that hire a large number of attorneys, such as the Federal Trade Commission, the Federal Communications Commission, the Federal Energy Regulatory Commission, the Nuclear Regulatory Commission, etc. One of the best sources for finding these internships is the University of Arizona's Government Honors and Internship Handbook, online at *www.law.arizona.edu/career/honorshandbook.cfm.* Another great source is the Leadership Directories (also known as the "Yellow Books"), which are published in print and online at *www.leadershipdirectories.com.* (Students should check with their law schools about online access using a password.) Once a student has interned at FERC, for example, that student can then write a compelling cover letter to those boutique firms that specialize in energy regulatory work and represent business clients before FERC.

An often overlooked category of entry-level jobs for graduating students is clerkships with Administrative Law Judges (ALJs). Over 31 federal agencies have ALJs. Clerking for an ALJ is a great way to gain expertise in a particular area and therefore become very marketable to boutique law firms. ALJs do not generally advertise their positions widely and, therefore, do not receive the same huge numbers of applicants as other federal judges. A list of ALJs with contact information can be found in *Want's Federal-State Court Directory*. You can also visit the website of the Federal Administrative Law Judge Conference, *www.faljc.org*.

The legal market in D.C., including the small- and medium-sized firms, is very competitive, but there are many opportunities. If students build their skills and focus their interests during law school, they can effectively target some of the sophisticated boutique law firms with unique D.C. practices.

Sheila Driscoll
Career Counselor
George Washington University Law School

➡ Focus on Indiana: Small by Number, Big by Reputation —

How a Small Indiana Law Firm Made a Name for Itself Taking on and Winning High-Stakes Lawsuits

The following article by Kelly Lucas is reprinted with permission from the June 30, 2004, Indiana Lawyer. *A fall 2003 survey by the Indiana State Bar Association revealed that 53.1% of Indiana's lawyers practice in law firms of five or fewer lawyers. More than 71% practice in firms comprising fewer than 15 lawyers.*

Scott Starr was the first person Jim Austen met when he entered Indiana University School of Law – Indianapolis. Starr, a second-year student, gave Austen a few pointers on how to navigate the law library. Today, while the stakes have become higher and the issues more complex, the two continue to provide counsel to one another when needed.

In the twenty-some years since the two graduated law school and hung out a collective shingle, they have given renewed meaning to the old adage, "It isn't the size of the dog in the fight, it's the size of the fight in the dog."

Starr and Austen, along with partners Donald Tribbett, Jon Myers, and Andrew Miller, and associate Stephanie Winkel, make up the Logansport law firm of Starr Austen Tribbett Myers & Miller. In recent years, members of the six-person legal team have faced off against a number of high-profile lawyers and law firms, winning substantial judgments and, in the process, earning a national reputation among litigators.

In 2002, Starr served as lead trial counsel in an Ohio class action securities case against Prudential Securities that resulted in compensatory and punitive damages in excess of $260 million. That was considered to be the seventh largest jury verdict rendered in the United States that year.

Austen recently had the opportunity to square off in federal court against Geoffrey Fieger. Fieger gained notoriety both in and outside the legal profession for his representation of Dr. Jack Kevorkian. In the process, Fieger earned a reputation as a lawyer who loves the limelight and has become a litigator that other lawyers look forward to challenging and, on rare occasion, defeating.

And that is what Austen did.

Bigger Not Always Better

In contrast to the plaintiff's verdict Starr and his team won on behalf of 300 retirees, Austen's defense case involved a civil rights lawsuit against a Mishawaka police officer. Both, however, debunk the "bigger is better" mindset.

In a small town you don't normally run across lawyers who get national publicity, Austen explained. Yet in this case, he found himself up against a lawyer who during the trial was doing evening interviews on a Fox News program.

"The thing that was unique for me was trying to trust my own instincts and not assume that because this guy is on national TV he must know more than I do," Austen said. What they've learned over the years is that it really doesn't matter whether you practice in a large or small firm. You just have to have some guts in this business, Austen added, and be willing to take some risks.

A Competitive Edge

Attitude alone doesn't get the job done, the lawyers caution. You have to spend money to make money.

When trying the Prudential case, the lawyers brought several jury consultants and technology firms onto their legal team. They were going up against California and Ohio firms with very good reputations in securities litigation, they said, and the stakes were high. That was part of the intrigue, Starr reveals, getting to do things the firm didn't ordinarily get to do.

A Los Angeles firm was hired to computerize the small courtroom in Marion, Ohio. All deposition pages were barcoded so if a witness testified on the stand differently than in deposition, the lawyers had the ability to bring the former contrary statement instantly on screen. They received assistance crafting the juror questionnaire, and a professional storyteller was even provided by one of the firms to help polish the presentation.

"He had incredibly insightful ideas, and he helped refine and structure the facts into a really compelling story," said Miller, who worked with Starr and other lawyers on the case. "In large part, the success of that case was driven by the fact that Scott did a great job of telling our story."

In retrospect, Miller said he expected a very sophisticated, slick presentation from Prudential's defense counsel, but the technological component of his team's presentation was light years ahead.

Big firm expectations are difficult to overcome, even when you are among the 71.1% of Indiana lawyers who practice in a firm of 15 lawyers or less.

The Prudential Securities case continues on appeal and, Miller concedes, the firm has been working on it for six years and has yet to receive a dime.

"But," Starr adds, "It will pay off." In the meantime, he said, the case has generated a number of referrals.

Running the Firm

Several things make Starr Austen Tribbett Myers & Miller unique in the small firm market. While they do some plaintiff's personal injury work, a very small percentage of their income comes from local business. Described as a general practice firm that concentrates heavily in litigation involving insurance defense, securities-related litigation, and complex commercial litigation including class actions, many of the lawyers spend a fair amount of time on the road.

One of the most noticeable things about the firm's office is the size of the support staff. The six-lawyer office employs ten secretaries and paralegals.

"When our big firm friends find out what our support staff-to-lawyer ratio is — here we have about two support staff for every lawyer — they find it hard to believe we can make a living with that ratio," Starr said. "But because of the nature of the practice and types of large and complex cases we handle, we have to have that support."

Having the level of support they do helps the firm keep fees low, Starr argues, because some work can be delegated from attorneys to paralegals.

The advantages to being a small firm in a small town are many, the lawyers say. The cost of living and the overhead of running a firm are substantially lower than in large cities. Lawyers with a lot on their plates can still drive home for dinner, make it to a child's ball game, and return to the office to put in a few more hours without considering whether a long commute in heavy traffic makes the trip worthwhile.

There is a downside, Starr adds. Attracting good quality, high-level young associates and convincing them that you can practice what many young lawyers perceive as "big firm lawyering" in a small town firm can be a challenge. That notion is perpetuated by many law schools, said Winkel, who recently came to the Logansport firm from Tampa, Florida, by a perception that the best go to the biggest firms.

Miller, who at 36 is the youngest of the five partners, said he has discovered that working in a firm of this size and in this location has made it much easier to strike a balance between his personal and professional lives. He feels more willing to put in the time at work, knowing he can be home in three minutes.

The partners say they will likely be adding another associate in the fall as a result of business growth.

While he understands where the big firm biases come from, Starr said, "I'll put our practice up against anybody's.

"I used to feel 15 years ago that we had a disadvantage in competing with big firms; I don't really feel that way anymore," Starr said. "We have lawyers from the big cities calling us and retaining us to represent their clients. As your reputation grows, big-firm bias becomes less of a concern."

IN THEIR OWN WORDS . . .

➡ Breaking into the Los Angeles Market

Los Angeles is a diverse and vibrant legal market that consists of firms of all sizes and practice areas. Because of the city's large geographic span, small firms can be found throughout the Los Angeles area. Most firms, however, are concentrated in the downtown area and on the Westside, which would include Beverly Hills, Santa Monica, Century City, and Westwood. In addition to offering the more conventional practice areas such as commercial litigation, corporate, bankruptcy, labor and employment, real estate, family law, environmental, and civil rights, to name just a few, Los Angeles firms are also known for their entertainment law specialization.

While a number of larger firms have an entertainment practice, there are many smaller entertainment law boutiques. These firms might represent clients on the studio side or often represent individual talent. Regardless of their client focus, it is extremely competitive to secure employment with them because of the number of attorneys who want to enter the field.

A majority of these firms do not recruit on campus nor do they hire entry-level attorneys or summer law clerks. Therefore, it is essential to make connections with the practitioners.

While networking through law school alumni and personal contacts is obviously important, there are other resources one can use to identify and meet entertainment attorneys. One bar association that has a particularly active entertainment law section is the Beverly Hills Bar Association (*www.bhba.org*). This section, which law students as well as attorneys can join, sponsors a variety of continuing legal education programs and other events. The Los Angeles County Bar *(www.lacba.org)* offers an entertainment law section as well, and lists firms with their practice areas in the Career portion of their website. Another resource useful for identifying entertainment firms is the *U.S. Directory of Entertainment Employers* from Studiolot Publishing.

Because Los Angeles is such a large and diverse city, it also offers a variety of active ethnic, gender-based, and specialty bar associations. These organizations play a critical role in facilitating connections among attorneys and making the networking process less overwhelming. The Women Lawyers Association of Los Angeles (*www.wlala.org*) sponsors many informational events as well as receptions. Other such associations include the Japanese American Bar Association of Greater Los Angeles (*www.jabaonline.org*), the Korean American Bar Association of Southern California (*www.kabasocal.org*), the Black Women Lawyers Association of Los Angeles (*www.blackwomenlawyersla.org*), the John M. Langston Bar Association (*www.jmlangston.org*), the Mexican American Bar Association (*www.mabalawyers.org*), the Southern California Chinese Lawyers Association (*www.sccla.org*), and the Lesbian and Gay Lawyers Association of Los Angeles (*www.lhr.org*). A comprehensive list of bar associations throughout California can be found on the California Bar website at *www.calbar.ca.gov.*

Amy Berenson Mallow
Assistant Dean for Career Services
UCLA School of Law

➡ Breaking into the New York City Market

The small firm market in New York City is psychologically eclipsed by the largest concentration of mega-firms in the country. It appears difficult for students to appreciate the rich variety and importance of small firm practice when the standard appears to be "size matters." Even those students denied entry into the large firms tend to disdain small firm practice. This is very unfortunate.

Because of its size, diverse population, and status as the world's financial center, New York City offers almost limitless opportunities for the smaller law firm in terms of practice, growth, and market share. Many of these practices are quite sophisticated. For example, I began life as a lawyer in a seven-attorney firm that represented two Fortune 500 companies. In addition, new lawyers in smaller firms usually enjoy immediate hands-on responsibilities. For this reason, many smaller firms will not recruit new associates until after the results of the bar examination, which in New York is rather late. This hiring timetable is so different from that of most larger firms that students tend to view the opportunities with small firms as "leftovers," failing to understand that the nature of small firm practice dictates the hiring timetable.

Tapping into the New York City small firm market is actually rather easy, although the sheer numbers can be daunting at first. Name your practice area and you will find it in countless firms, either in specialized "boutiques" or in general practice firms. Developing a list of such firms using the MarHub directory of LexisNexis® is very easy; students should contact their career services office for instructions. Because small firms cannot afford to experiment with associate hires, clerking for them during the summer and/or during the academic year is extremely important. Unlike in the large firms, there is usually no expectation of a permanent offer, but in the event that the firm wants to hire an associate, the student with the track record will most likely get the nod.

It is important for students to understand that firm size is relative to population size. A small firm in New York City can be, and often is, a large firm in another locale. And if one lived in that other locale, the firm would be sought after for its size and practice, whereas the same size firm is not sought after in New York City, although the firm may well be, and probably is, practicing at the same sophistication level.

Joan King
Director of Career Services
Brooklyn Law School

➡ Breaking into the San Francisco Market

The City By The Bay is a very popular destination for law students and recent graduates. It is far easier to seek opportunities with small firms once you are actually in San Francisco. Local employers are notorious for asking prospective candidates about their connection to the city. Your presence not only indicates that you are committed to working in San Francisco but that you are aware of the cost of living and are still committed to working in San Francisco.

San Francisco attorneys are very active in a number of local specialty and minority bar associations. In addition to reduced student membership rates, there are many opportunities to attend continuing legal education programs full of attorneys. Among the most popular local bar associations are: The Bar Association of San Francisco (frequently referred to as BASF) (*www.sfbar.org*), the San Francisco Trial Lawyers Association (*www.sftla.org*), the Queen's Bench (supporting and promoting women in the profession) (*www.queensbench.org*), the California Employment Lawyers Association (*www.celaweb.org*), and the Asian American Bar Association of the Greater Bay Area (*www.aaba-bay.com*). The San Francisco Intellectual Property Law Association (*www.sfipla.org*) is very active and holds an annual job fair in early August.

While there are 14,740 active attorneys in San Francisco, it truly is a "small" legal community. The legal community here is very tight-knit and in this diverse and progressive city you can never predict who may have the connection that will lead to your next job. The value of networking cannot be underestimated. Personal referrals will go a long way, and first impressions may last a lifetime. Local attorneys, as well as their friends and families, are often involved in community volunteer work.

A few of the many civic opportunities available are: Hands on Bay Area (*www.communityimpact.org*), the Golden Gate National Park Recreation Area volunteer program (*www.nps.gov/goga/vip/*), and for those athletes or aspiring athletes the Leukemia and Lymphoma Society of Northern California has a thriving Team in Training program (*www.teamintraining.org*). In addition, there are many local nonprofits that often seek additional volunteers for their Boards. (See *www.compasspoint.org* for nonprofit Board opportunities.)

The *Recorder* (*www.callaw.com*) and the *Daily Journal* (*www.dailyjournal.com*) are San Francisco's local weekday legal publications. They both contain job listings and are available online. In the words of author James Michener, "The extreme geniality of San Francisco's economic, intellectual, and political climate makes it the most varied and challenging city in the United States." As such, there is a lot of value in keeping abreast of current events. *The Chronicle*, and its online version SFGate (*www.sfgate.com*), is the largest local daily newspaper. Craigslist (*www.craigslist.org*), founded in San Francisco, is another valuable resource for job listings, apartments, and local events.

Many candidates are aware that San Francisco is in the "Bay Area" but they often do not realize the number of opportunities that lie outside of the City. Think regionally when you are relocating to Northern California: Investigate opportunities in the North Bay (Marin, Napa, and Sonoma counties), East Bay (Alameda, Contra Costa), South Bay (San Mateo county), and the Peninsula (Santa Clara county). It is also worth expanding your search even further to Sacramento, Humboldt, Fresno, or Kern county, where the market is less competitive.

Lisa Dickinson
Director of Career Services
University of San Francisco School of Law

Targeting Rural Markets

I am writing as a practitioner from a small state largely made up of small towns with small firms in them. There are some differences in the way firms hire between those in what I would call a small town (10,000 or more population) and what I would think of as a rural area (anything less than 10,000 residents). But in some respects they have much in common.

Both rural and small town firms are apt to contact the law school for help recruiting. The rural firm may not contact the career services office (CSO), opting instead for familiar professors or the dean. This happens with small town firms also, but to a lesser degree. With luck, the faculty member or dean will alert the CSO to the firm's needs, and the CSO will convince the firm to post a notice for interested students. Absent that luck, the student is dependent on a faculty member or the dean knowing that he or she is interested in a rural or small town practice.

Rural firms, even more than those in small towns, are justifiably skeptical of a student who answers a job posting but is not from the vicinity. Laterals tend to move into rural areas for reasons other than the job, so the risk of hiring is much less for the firm. The risk to the firm is that a student naively wants a job, any job, and will leave after a year of professional and personal boredom.

What does this mean for students who want to practice in a small town or rural area? It means the primary issue to the employers is the student's commitment to the area and, as a corollary, commitment to the firm. Firms will not accept your commitment to the position unless they believe you are both serious and knowledgeable about living in their community. Rather than high academic achievement, these firms look for people skills, the ability to work with clients and community, and well-informed applicants. Of course, one must have passing grades, a law degree, and be admitted or able to become admitted to the state bar. But when basic academic requirements are met, the person reading your cover letter wants to know why you would come to this small, rural community to start your legal career. Your answer must be more than a cliché about the holistic benefits of general practice, the friendly pace of small town life, good schools, etc.

Before approaching these firms, do your research. What is the economic base of the town? How close is it to a larger metropolitan area? Who makes up the firm's client list? Are any significant changes occurring — increasing or decreasing growth or land values, a four-lane highway in the future, a factory to be closed or opened, turmoil in the local government? What is the socio-economic and socio-cultural picture of the area? Is it a high- or low-income area, a homogeneous population, or a highly stratified community? What is the pattern of growth?

How do you get this information? Your librarian may help you find area newspapers and state government agency reports. Find out if the town or local newspaper has a website. Ascertain if there is a Chamber of Commerce or local bar association. Search the statewide or regional newspapers for information on the town (or the law firm). Many newspapers are searchable in full text on Westlaw® or LexisNexis®.

Most importantly, talk to people from the area. If you are attending law school in-state, check with the career services office to find any students from the locale. Find out why they do or do not want to return to the area after graduating. Perhaps they will know of this firm and can provide background on the members. Find out what sections of the state bar association the members of the firm are involved with. Use this information to contact other section members you may know, or those who are graduates of your law school, and get information about the firm from them. In small states, many lawyers in larger towns are good sources of information on smaller communities. Use the contacts you already have through the local bar. In a state like Arkansas, with fewer than 8,000 licensed attorneys, you may be surprised how well acquainted practicing lawyers are with their counterparts throughout the state. Finally, before going too far, check with the licensing authority of the state to determine if the firm, or its members, have a record of ethical sanctions.

Once you have researched the community and the firm, start contacting the firms. There are two types of job search contacts. One is the reply to an advertised position. Since these are rare in rural areas, the other contact, that seeking information, is more widely used for a rural job search. In either case your "informed commitment" to the area, and therefore to the law firm, overrides virtually all else. Before setting out to uncover the "hidden rural job market" you must decide which places to target, and why. Be flexible. Don't concentrate on one area only. Identify a handful of areas and keep your eyes open for opportunities elsewhere. When you can state why you want to make the area your home, start your search in earnest by planning a visit. Precede the visit by contacting the lawyers, attempting to schedule your stops to include meetings with both firms. (It is a commonly known truism that a small town must have at least two law firms to keep each other in business. More than that often gluts the market.) During your visit, include the following as preliminary to your meetings with the lawyers:

1. **The courthouse.** Introduce yourself to the clerks and let them know you are considering relocation to the area. Have business cards with you and ask for theirs. Visit the local judges, introduce yourself, and explain what you are doing. Ask judges which lawyers you should talk to about opportunities in the area. Ask the clerk which firms are run well, or are busy and might need assistance.

2. **A realtor.** Inquire about housing in the region. Ask for directions to drive through residential areas and pick up any listing magazines that may be available.

3. **The bank.** One can often get a sense of a small, rural town by catching the "feel" of the bank lobby, particularly if there is only one. It is probably on the square and near the best café in town. Pick up the bank's account literature and go across the street for a meal at the café. You will get a better feel for the town from that café than from any other place with the possible exception of the post office or gas station. We really are talking rural here!

4. **A church or synagogue**, if you are a believer. If you can arrange to attend services, so much the better. Many social functions are supported by the faith community, and this can be especially true in rural areas.

5. **The law firms and lawyers.** These visits should be arranged in advance if possible. Write a letter, follow up with a telephone call, and let them know when you will be in town. Do NOT ask for a job. Simply ask for the opportunity to visit and get advice on relocation to the area. Regardless of whether you like the firm, follow your visit with a thank you note. If you do like the firm, offer to provide research assistance for a reasonable fee if needed. Remember, what is "reasonable" in a rural area may be different than the normal scale where you are. This is an opportunity to demonstrate your value and become acquainted with the local practice. Be sure your research is prompt, efficient, and accurate. Get clear instructions on how much time to spend and bill only to the agreed amount. If the firm decides a new associate is needed, you will be a likely candidate. If not, you will at least get to know the "other side" in a friendly, professional manner.

If a personal visit to the area is out of the question, contact letters to law firms must take the place of face-to-face visits. The offer of research assistance is always an excellent introduction, and often a welcome resource for a small town firm.

Do not be discouraged when told there are no openings for a new attorney. Many small firms have no comprehension of the need for a new attorney until the right person comes along and becomes indispensable. Maintain contact with the firms you are interested in. As with so many areas of human enterprise, taking the initiative and starting early gives you a double advantage over those who merely wait for something to come their way. The more persistent and focused you are, the better your efforts will pay off.

Claudia Driver
formerly Director of Career Services
and Continuing Legal Education
University of Arkansas School of Law
Fayetteville, AK

CHAPTER 3:

Getting Hired

"Fall seven times, stand up eight."

JAPANESE PROVERB

Once you secure an interview with an employer, you are very close to being offered a job. Contrary to popular belief, no one (particularly not small firms with limited time for recruiting) invites a candidate to interview out of pity or error. You have been selected based upon your paper credentials and, if you are connecting through others, as a result of your networking acumen.

Qualities to Emphasize

Students want to know if there is some magic formula that employers use when making hiring decisions. A single magic formula, alas, does not exist. However, based upon conversations with hundreds of hiring partners over the years, I can tell you that intelligence, a demonstrable work ethic, and motivation for practicing the kind of law the firm engages in are the three immutable characteristics of a desirable candidate. Let's review each of these characteristics and see how you can incorporate these qualities in your next interview.

● Intelligence

As one employer put it bluntly to a recent job candidate: "Are you smart?" (This is a true story, and the answer ought to have been, "Yes, I am really smart.")

Intelligence comes in a variety of forms, and you need to describe your own personal brand of intelligence in terms that a small firm lawyer will appreciate. Among the most marketable forms are excellent written skills, verbal communication skills, organizational skills, or advocacy skills. Employers want to hire people with intelligence and good judgment, not necessarily MENSA members. Good grades, as you might discern from some of your classmates on Law Review, are not necessarily indicative of intelligence and good judgment. Grades and class rank are used as indicators at larger law firms because of the high volume of résumés they receive and the need to screen credentials quickly. Good grades, however, don't tell the entire story, and employers (including the big firms) know this.

Even if your grades are less than stellar, think about ways you've excelled in law school and college and describe them clearly to your interviewer. For example, your first semester grades were disappointing, but you are a Moot Court champion. Perhaps your timed exams resulted in poor grades, but your legal writing grade demonstrates a strong aptitude for research and drafting. Sometimes students excel in clinics and show strong interpersonal skills and a gift for client relations. Find your strengths and highlight them for employers. If you're having trouble pinning down your strengths, talk to your professors or classmates for some insight. Sometimes a disinterested third party can zero in on your intellectual gifts.

In addition to intellectual intelligence, emotional intelligence has gained recognition as a strong component of a successful person. Superior intellect does not translate into instantaneous professional success, particularly if you lack the all-important people skills. Think about some of the folks on the Law Review who are geniuses but can't seem to navigate life's inevitable ups and downs.

● **Work Ethic**

Law is a tough business with long hours and high stress levels. It requires dedication, attention to detail, and focus. Employers want to see a strong, demonstrable work ethic. Simply going to law school does not qualify you as having a strong work ethic. Nor does a J.D. degree entitle you to the job of your dreams. The degree is simply a prerequisite in most jurisdictions for practicing law.

So, how do you show a strong desire to work hard? Talk about prior work experiences that required long hours and focus. Think about part-time jobs you held in conjunction with school responsibilities. Discuss summer jobs you held, legal and non-legal, in which you were responsible and hardworking. Provide your interviewer with a list of references of people, preferably law professors or former legal employers, who will attest to your dedication and responsibility.

➡ Who Gets Hired?

Do grades matter in the small firm setting? They absolutely do. However, grades need not be the most important decision in small firm hiring. In addition to grades, people skills, the ability to think fast, and your potential for bringing in business may all make you attractive to a small firm employer.

First and foremost are people skills. In a small office setting, it is not possible to turn irate, angry, or upset clients over to another person. There is often no one else. It is important to be able to converse and function within several layers of society. In any given day I can speak with everyone from well-educated, quick-witted lawyers, to sharp businessmen and convicted felon junkies. If they are clients, they must all believe I respect them, I understand them, and I am trying my hardest to help them.

The small firm often provides opportunities for quick wit and the ability to think on your feet. In a small firm it is possible that you may be the only one available when a major case comes in. While working at my last firm, my employer was on vacation out of the country for ten days and I was the only one in the office. I was in charge. On the second day of his vacation, a corporate client called to report that he had just been arrested. Though our firm handled very few criminal matters, I knew that we would handle this because of the existing relationship. A few minutes into the telephone call I learned the arrest involved an attempted murder! There was nowhere to seek guidance; the decisions were mine.

Finally, in my first position out of law school, I applied to a small boutique firm. The firm typically employed students with a significantly higher GPA than mine. During the interview process, I indicated I would be willing to take a salary of approximately half the firm's typical starting salary in exchange for a significant percentage of the business I brought in. At the end of my first year I had done somewhat better than attorneys with more tenure. Additionally, I was able to obtain a position that might otherwise have been out of my reach.

James K. Rubin, Esq.
The Law Offices of James K. Rubin, P.A.
North Miami Beach, Florida

● **Motivation to Work at that Particular Firm**

Everybody wants to feel special and loved. Lawyers are no different. A potential employer wants to feel that you are interested in them because they are a wonderful place to practice law — not simply because you need a job.

Focus on your strengths and be ready to discuss them with your interviewer. Do not presume that "your résumé speaks for itself." Your résumé is simply a piece of paper with your relevant credentials. It will not magically come to life on the interviewer's desk and begin advocating for you. You need to advocate for yourself in the interview. Help to connect your skills with the needs of the firm.

One way to demonstrate your motivation to work at that particular firm is to ask questions during and at the end of the interview. Typically, at the end of most interviews the employer will ask if you have any questions. This is most decidedly not the time to sit silently and hope for the best. Ask questions that demonstrate your interest in working at the firm. Here are a few never-fail questions to pose to an interviewer:

- ✓ Why did you decide to practice law at a smaller firm?
- ✓ What do you enjoy about your work as an attorney?
- ✓ What qualities are the most important to you in selecting an entry-level associate?

These questions are good because they are open-ended and allow you to respond with positive information about yourself. Here's a sample of a question-and-answer dialogue to help you see how good questions can help further your case:

- ✓ *Interviewee:* What are the top qualities you seek in an entry-level associate?

- ✓ *Interviewer:* We really want someone who can work independently and who understands the business of law.

- ✓ *Interviewee:* That makes a lot of sense. You know, when I worked in the Health Law Clinic, I was a Certified Legal Intern and was solely responsible for handling three client files. I found that it was really satisfying to counsel someone and help them find a solution. I feel that it prepared me for private practice at a smaller firm where I know there is less programmatic mentoring. I'm ready to hit the ground running.

Articulate your interest in working at the firm. It's a mistake to assume that simply showing up for the interview conveys your desire to work at the firm. Assuming that you really want to work at a particular firm where you are interviewing, it is perfectly all right to say words to this effect: "I really enjoyed speaking with you. You know, if you were to make me an offer, I would gladly accept and be able to begin working on September 1 after the bar exam." Here's another strategy to demonstrate motivation and interest: "I really want to join this firm and work with you. Would it help you to make a decision if you could contact former employers or faculty members?" Be prepared with a list of references for the convenience of the employer.

Not only do your words demonstrate your motivation and energy, but so does your body language. Be aware of how you sound and how you present yourself. For example:

✓ Sit up straight and tall in your chair — don't slouch.

✓ Make eye contact with the interviewer. Meandering eyes convey a lack of interest.

✓ Smile. Too many students feel that an interview is a serious situation (which it is!), but translate that to mean that they need to appear grim. Laugh, when appropriate, and smile. Be careful with offbeat humor — avoid deploying dry wit, particularly if there is a chance that it will be misconstrued.

✓ Shake hands at the beginning of the interview and at the end.

TEN TIPS FOR IMPRESSING AN INTERVIEWER

1. **Be prepared.** Every grizzled interviewer will tell you that nothing kills an interview faster than a candidate who is clueless about the firm. Do some basic research before the interview and come prepared with information about the firm and the interviewer.

2. **Dress for success.** Appearance matters, so dress to impress. Keep attire conservative. Learn if the firm is in business casual mode and dress accordingly. Pay attention to basic grooming. Avoid perfume or strong colognes.

3. **Be on time.** Don't saunter in ten minutes after the appointed time. Know the location of the firm, figure out travel time, and budget for traffic or other unforeseen delays.

4. **Treat everyone with respect.** Don't strut into the waiting room and treat the receptionist with contempt. Support staff are indispensable in all firms, and in smaller firms they may even have input in the hiring process. Don't blow your chances of being hired by being a clown in the waiting room.

5. **Bring supporting documents.** Have extra copies of your résumé, transcript, recommendation letters, list of references, and writing sample on hand just in case. Be ready to supply pertinent documentation to your interviewer.

6. **Anticipate objections.** Be prepared to answer those difficult questions that no one likes to confront, such as a really bad grade in a course, a prior work experience that did not end well, or a lack of experience in a particular practice area. While you should not bring up your shortcomings, you should anticipate possible objections. Rehearse through mock interviews with someone you know.

7. **Listen, listen, listen.** Listen to what your interviewer is saying and affirm his or her words. Be engaged in the process and respond appropriately.

8. **Advocate for yourself.** Don't fall into the trap of thinking "your résumé speaks for itself." You need to be an advocate. Tell the employer about specific skills or experiences that relate to the job you are seeking. Do not be shy about describing your accomplishments.

9. **Ask questions.** Be prepared with some substantive questions to ask the interviewer. At the end of most interviews, you can expect to be asked, "Do you have any questions for me?" Being unprepared will make you appear to be disinterested.

10. **Say "thank you."** Thank the interviewer in person for his or her time. Then write or e-mail a thank you letter memorializing your visit. This is not only good manners but shows that you are interested.

Dress for Success

Each day, we present ourselves to the outside world and our appearances affect how we are perceived by others. Our clothes, hair, makeup, and demeanor all signal strong messages to the world about who we are and what we are about. Countless studies confirm what we all know: first impressions count. An outstanding résumé with the best of credentials will be derailed by a sloppy personal appearance or poor interview skills.

The day before you travel to an interview, confirm with the employer (whether through the secretary or attorney) and determine the dress code. Even if the office is "all casual, all the time," your best bet is to arrive for each interview in traditional business attire, unless very specifically instructed otherwise. Far better to show your most professional appearance to a potential employer than to seem less than completely focused on presenting yourself and the firm in the best possible light. There will be time enough to enjoy the relaxed work environment of your employer after you've gotten the job.

- **Traditional Business Dress**

Traditional business dress for men means a suit, usually in a dark fabric, a white shirt, tie, and dress shoes. There will be regional differences in attire that you should be attuned to. If you are unsure, a visit to a department store will help allay your fears and ensure that you arrive properly attired for the interview. For women, traditional dress entails a suit with a skirt or pantsuit, a muted blouse, pantyhose, and mid-height heels.

For resources discussing casual and traditional attire, see the Appendix beginning on page 150.

- **Casual Dress**

Casual dress at law firms has grown largely out of a desire on the part of each firm to create a work environment in harmony with its clients. As high-technology start-ups, with their "24-7" work days and relaxed, informal atmospheres, became successful businesses, their cultures spread to their professional service providers and throughout the economy.

The definition of casual dress will differ from firm to firm. Typically, casual dress codes dictate open-collared shirts (such as polo shirts or button-downs, no T-shirts allowed), casual trousers such as khakis, and casual shoes such as loafers or moccasins with socks (open-toed shoes are often discouraged, sometimes for workplace safety reasons). Forbidden items include anything you would wear to do yard work, such as tennis shoes, sandals, halter or tank tops, jeans, sweat-pants, or shorts.

Most major department stores and clothing bou-tiques will offer free advice and, perhaps, have a per-sonal shopper on staff to assist you. Many designers have created entire lines dedicated to casual dress attire. Men will probably want at least three pairs of tailored khaki trousers and several casual shirts. A blazer is a worthwhile purchase as well for those casual but somewhat more formal client meetings and for the unexpected trip to a nice restaurant. Invest in a good pair of casual business shoes; again, many shoe manufacturers now offer entire lines of casual dress shoes. For women, department stores and national chains offer good examples of appropriate casual business attire.

● Grooming

Appropriate grooming is essential to your professional image. I emphasize the word "appropriate" since there is no Platonic ideal for what constitutes the right look. Some advice books will vow that facial hair is out of the question; others will warn against long hair. It's important to be yourself and to present the best groomed version of yourself to an employer. Do not radically change your style to conform to a particular job, particularly if it means acting in a deceptive manner. After all, you are not likely to be happy in a job that does not allow you to be yourself.

Consider the region in which you are interviewing when you think about grooming choices. In some parts of the country, moustaches and longer hair are definitely "out" for men. You should be aware of the grooming trends in the area where you are seeking employment and decide if you want to conform. This is absolutely your choice, but it might ease your way into the job of your dreams.

NINE COMMON-SENSE GROOMING TIPS

1. **Cleanliness *is* next to godliness.** Be sure you shower and wear deodorant on interview day.

2. **If you have long hair, consider pulling it back so it doesn't hang in your face.** You don't have to cut off the Rapunzel-length locks, but do consider various styles that look professional.

3. **Keep jewelry to a minimum.** It can be distracting to shake hands with someone loaded with bangle bracelets.

4. **If you have body parts other than your earlobes pierced, keep it to yourself.** Ditto for tattoos.

5. **Avoid wearing strong or excessive perfume or cologne on interview day.** Sometimes, particularly in the close confines of an interview room, the scent can become overwhelming.

6. **Look at your hands.** Are they mangled from nervous nail biting or picking? Your hands are among the first things an employer will notice. Make sure they look well-groomed. Women should avoid dark polish colors and stick with neutral shades instead.

7. **Shine your shoes.** Buy an inexpensive polish kit and make sure your shoes sparkle. You don't have to buy the most expensive shoes, but they should be clean and in good repair.

8. **Women should wear conservative makeup.** The Goth Look is definitely out for interviews. At a minimum, wear lipstick, mascara, and blush.

9. **Practice good dental hygiene** — brush your teeth!

- **Professionalism**

    You are a professional from the moment you begin law school. A professional adheres to the highest standard of conduct in all matters related to work. Professionalism means that your cover letter and résumé are free of typographical errors and are truthful. Professionalism means that you show up on time for an interview and are attired appropriately for the occasion. Professionals keep their word and behave ethically throughout the hiring process, adhering to timing deadlines and communicating clearly.

    NALP — The Association for Legal Career Professionals — publishes *Principles and Standards for Law Placement and Recruitment Activities.* (See the Appendix on page 161 for more information or visit *www.nalp.org* for the full text of the *Principles and Standards.*) Specifically, Part V (A)(1) provides that offers to law students should remain open for at least two weeks after the date made. Further, Part V(A)(6) provides that "Employers having a total of 40 attorneys or fewer in all offices ... should leave offers open for a minimum of three weeks." The *Principles and Standards* are ethical guidelines applying to the recruitment of law students, not to lateral hires.

    Demonstrate your professionalism throughout your job search by:

    ✓ Communicating clearly with a prospective employer about timing of offers and acceptances.

    ✓ Keeping your word once you agree to a timeline.

    ✓ Making sure that your correspondence is typed and error-free.

✓ Representing your credentials truthfully.

✓ Accepting an offer and then declining all subsequent interview opportunities. (If you are holding an additional offer at the point you accept a job, be prompt in declining the other offer.)

✓ Maintaining your integrity throughout the interview process will benefit you both in the short-term and the long run. In the short-term, you will exude a professional demeanor and be able to communicate clear expectations in terms of timelines. In the long run, your reputation will precede you in the local legal community. Not surprisingly, lawyers talk to one another and a bad experience with a law student or recent graduate will be communicated to others and will, ultimately, tarnish your reputation.

➡️ **What to Expect from the Small Law Firm Interview**

The hiring of attorneys is among the most important decisions that a law firm will make, and has a direct effect on the profitability and culture of the firm. This is particularly true of small firms with few attorneys, where each attorney has more "visibility" than he or she would have in a larger firm. Although interviewing for a position with a small law firm is similar in many respects to interviewing with larger firms or other organizations, there are some differences that are helpful to keep in mind.

Because of the importance of a small law firm's hiring decisions and the cost of a bad decision, many small firms place increased emphasis on the interviewing process. They tend to take their time in choosing the appropriate candidate and to pay close attention to all of the information that they gather regarding the candidate. The well-prepared candidate should be prepared for the following when embarking on interviews with small firms:

- Interviews may be lengthy and/or numerous, as the attorneys are trying to "size you up" and see whether you would be a good fit for the firm, both in terms of experience/skill and personality. The candidate may be interviewed during different times of day and by all or most of the attorneys at the firm.

- The firm may go out of its way to engage in dialogue with the candidate to determine if his or her thought processes and experiences are consistent with the firm. This may include discussion of some of the cases or matters that the candidate has worked on, as well as the types of cases/matters that the firm would have the candidate working on.

- The firm may ask the candidate to do a test project, designed specifically for the position and requiring a modest time commitment. Not only will the firm be judging the candidate's skill, but also his or her timeliness and commitment.

- The firm may be particularly interested in learning whether the candidate is able to multitask, and whether he or she is someone who has the desire for and ability to handle significant responsibility at an early level.

- The firm will likely want to discuss billable hour requirements, both to set expectations and to determine whether expectations are consistent. In addition, the firm may attempt to assess the candidate's work ethic to ensure that it is consistent with the overall work ethic at the firm.

Remember that this is a two-sided process. Just as the small firm is gathering as much information as it can regarding the prospective candidate, the candidate should likewise use the interviewing process to learn as much as it can about the firm in order to ensure a "good fit." Although an attorney's skills are, of course, of primary importance, an attorney's success within a small firm depends in large part on his or her compatibility with the other attorneys at the firm.

Alan M. Tarter
Managing Partner
Tarter Krinsky & Drogin LLP*

Debra Bodian Bernstein
Associate
Tarter Krinsky & Drogin LLP*

* Tarter Krinsky & Drogin LLP has offices in New York City and Princeton, New Jersey.

CHAPTER 4:

Succeeding at a Small Firm

"Energy and persistence conquer all things."

BENJAMIN FRANKLIN

After interviewing with a small firm and receiving an offer of employment, the path toward career success now opens. This chapter will discuss the salary negotiation process and offer some tips to help you negotiate a fair compensation package. Later on, you will learn how to succeed on a day-to-day basis and avoid common roadblocks to success. Finally, we will conclude with a discussion of the partnership timeline at small firms.

Strategies for Negotiating Salary and Benefits

Unlike larger law firms that hire many entry-level and lateral associate candidates each year, a small firm may hire a new lawyer only once a year — or even less frequently. Therefore, small firms may not be as savvy about prevailing salaries, billable hour requirements, and benefits. This means that part of your responsibility in the negotiating process is to know what lawyers are making in your geographic area and to have a reasonable expectation about what a small firm can afford to pay. Researching and gathering information prior to meeting with partners will help you in the negotiation process.

● **Salary Considerations**

Salary statistics for small firms are difficult to ascertain since there is little statistical reporting, unlike larger firms that routinely report starting salaries to the public. The NALP *2004 Associate Salary Survey* reported a $65,000 median first-year starting salary for associates at firms between 2 and 25 lawyers — and a $72,900 median first-year associate salary for firms with between 26 and 50 lawyers.

Since small firm salaries will vary from region to region, it is important for you to gather information from several sources. Talk to your career services office, the local bar association, or practitioners you know to learn about salary ranges in your area for smaller firms. You should also consult salary surveys by national organizations such as NALP, Altman Weil, and the *National Law Journal*. Keep in mind that large national studies may not reflect local realities.

After you gather some threshold information, assess your reasonable financial needs following graduation. "Reasonable" is the operative word here. Do not expect to graduate from law school and buy a Jaguar. For example, ask yourself:

✓ If you have student loans, what can you expect your monthly payments to be? A visit to your

Financial Aid Office will help you gather this information.

✓ Do you have other debts to pay? Consider car loans, mortgages and consumer credit card debts.

✓ What are your current monthly living expenses? Do you expect them to rise, diminish, or stay about the same following graduation?

✓ What post-graduate expenses do you anticipate? Think about the bar examination and any preparatory courses you might take. A larger apartment? Some new career clothes to wear to court?

Once you have a handle on your reasonable financial needs, you can discern what a reasonable salary would be in order to meet your financial goals.

When approaching a salary negotiation session, find the negotiating strategy that works best for you. Dozens of books are available (see the Appendix for a list of salary negotiating resources) and you should become familiar with different styles of negotiating. One method of salary negotiation involves slightly overstating your salary needs with the assumption that the hiring attorney will bargain down as a matter of course. For example, if you know you need to make at least $45,000 in order to pay your student loans and consumer debt, rent a one-bedroom apartment, buy a used car to commute to the office, and have reasonable living expenses, then you might want to ask for $48,000.

- **Benefits**

    Small law firms will offer a range of benefits depending on a variety of factors. The following is a list of benefits that a small firm may provide to an associate:

    ✓ Medical insurance for you and/or your dependents.

    ✓ Dental insurance for you and/or your dependents.

    ✓ Vision insurance for you and/or your dependents.

    ✓ 401(k) or other contributory savings plans.

    ✓ Flexible spending plans.

    ✓ Parking.

    ✓ Employee Assistance Plan ("EAP") for confidential mental health counseling.

    ✓ Bar membership (national, state, and/or local).

    ✓ Summer stipend in order to study for the bar or limited part-time work prior to the bar examination to defray costs.

    ✓ Professional license fees (state).

    ✓ Continuing legal education classes.

    ✓ Vacation.

    ✓ Maternity/paternity leave.

    ✓ Sick and personal days.

    Benefits will vary from firm to firm; not all firms can or will provide all of the benefits listed above. Knowing the local market will assist you in negotiating the best deal, so be sure to ask practitioners, bar association officials, or career services professionals for their take on reasonable benefits for your market.

● Billable Hours

Lawyers typically bill clients on the basis of the number of hours worked on a particular matter. For lawyers, time — literally — is money. So, it's important for you to know what the billable hours requirement is at your small firm. This number will vary from firm to firm depending upon economic goals, type of clients, and hourly fees. You should understand from the outset what your employer's expectations are and be prepared to honor those expectations. In addition to establishing the threshold billable hours requirements, you might want to ask:

✓ Are certain activities exempt from billable hours, such as *pro bono* work or recruiting activities?

✓ What are the firm's policies regarding timesheets? Do you have to complete a timesheet daily, weekly, or monthly?

✓ Does the firm offer bonuses on the basis of billable hours? What are the policies underlying bonuses?

● When to Walk Away

Receiving an offer of employment should be cause for celebration. However, if during the course of salary negotiations you find yourself in an untenable position, either financially or in fulfilling your professional expectations of what your work life should look like, then you might have to consider walking away from the offer. Assess the warning signs before you accept an offer:

✓ Your "gut reaction" is that this firm is not well-regarded in the community and that you will not receive the kind of training and professional mentoring that will assist you in your next job search.

✓ The firm experiences an enormous amount of associate turnover. No one seems to stay very long.

✓ You are totally disinterested in the firm's practice areas and would not be engaged by the kind of work they do.

✓ The firm is located in a geographic location that is not convenient or would require relocation and you would prefer not to relocate.

✓ The salary offer is so low that you would not be able to pay off your student loans and have a reasonable standard of living.

✓ You do not connect with the attorneys and do not feel that you would fit in well at the firm.

Employment always involves risks and rewards, and you should expect to compromise on some issues. If the risks clearly override any possible rewards, then you should consider declining an offer and redoubling your efforts to find the right job for you. Declining an offer is risky, but in some cases it is the right thing to do. You need to ask yourself whether a better position looms on the horizon or if you risk a prolonged job search.

Fostering Excellence in Practice

Becoming an excellent associate, a valued and esteemed employee, is rather like putting together a jigsaw puzzle. There are several pieces to assemble: excellent work product, fulfillment of billable hours requirements, an effort at client-getting, fostering client relations, and the ability to work independently, to name a few. Before you begin work, you should be familiar with the expectations of your employer. Every employer will emphasize different factors. For some, excellent work product is valued above all else, and client-getting is addressed later in your professional development. At other firms, fulfilling the billable hours requirement is highly prized to the exclusion of some of the other factors. Learn what behavior will be rewarded and aim to foster excellence in those areas.

- **Excellent Work Product**

Most seasoned practitioners will agree that entry-level lawyers need to work on the fundamentals of creating consistently excellent work products for clients. This translates into memoranda, pleadings, and contracts that are well-written, concise, accurate, and well-researched. No matter how well you present yourself or how well liked you may be, if you do not have the substantive skills, then it is unlikely that you will succeed in the long run.

When you first begin your new job, ask if the firm uses any model pleadings or if a file of model pleadings exists. Rather than reinvent the wheel with each assignment, it can help to have model pleadings for guidance. At the start of your work, it might also be helpful to find an attorney, preferably an associate, who can briefly review your initial assignments to ensure that your work conforms to the firm's general style.

Know the timeline for every assignment and keep your promises. Tardy assignments, even if they are ultimately good work product, will reflect poorly on you. If you are juggling several assignments, prioritize and keep to your schedule. If you ask an attorney when an assignment is due and you receive a vague answer ("whenever you think it's complete"), either press for a certain time or make your own deadline and stick to it ("I should complete this within one week, if that sounds right to you"). Small firms prize self-starters who are able to assume work responsibilities and complete assignments in a timely manner.

- **Billable Hours**

Lawyers make money by billing for time spent on a case or deal. Time equals money. Therefore, time-keeping becomes an important litmus test for determining whether or not you are a profitable asset to the firm.

Firms will have different billable hours policies. Some firms will state a minimum billable hours requirement for the year. This will range from 1,600 billable hours per year (which is on the low end) to 2,400 billable hours per year and up (which is on the high end). Take into account what activities constitute billable hours and what do not. Some activities, such as *pro bono* or bar association work, might not count into your firm's billable hours requirements. Your firm might circulate time reports to assess your billable hours pace for the year. If your firm does not create pace reports to track your progress, then you should keep tabs on your progress to make sure that you are reaching your stated annual goal. This will prevent you from being ambushed at year's end with an impossible goal. Know the policy and make every effort to reach the billable hours target.

Know the firm's policy for submitting timesheets and follow procedures precisely. Ask if timesheets are due at the end of each day, week, or month. Do not shortchange yourself by minimizing hours or violate ethical rules by overstating your hours. Get into the habit of keeping time contemporaneously with the events of the day. It might help to have a desk clock so that you can chart your progress. Ideally, you should keep your timesheet next to your telephone and refer to it often during the day to capture all your billable hours. Lawyers who try to recreate timesheets often underestimate hours spent on a project or recollect inaccurately the events of the day.

Learn the system for recording time from the firm's billing assistant, office manager, or experienced secretaries. If there are certain common abbreviations used by your firm, use them. Write clearly and in sufficient detail in the event that you need to recall an assignment later. Bear in mind that your written description of the work you perform is often transmitted directly to the client as part of the firm's invoice; use good sense in describing your work.

• Client-Getting

Clients are the lifeblood of any firm. Without clients, hours cannot be billed and collected, and the business fails. Discuss client-getting with an experienced attorney of the firm and understand the firm's expectations as they relate to you. Know if the firm values client-getting at an early stage in your professional career, or if they would prefer that you focus solely on professional skills development.

Inquire about the firm's target clients. Some firms have business plans that outline the ideal clients who are most suited to the expertise of the firm's lawyers. For example, if a firm practices primarily in the area of plaintiffs' personal injury law, it might not be helpful to solicit a client with a complex estate administration problem that requires extensive knowledge of the Internal Revenue Code. If you know your quarry, you can target potential clients that will complement the firm's business.

Ask about how the firm helps to encourage client-getting activities. If you have a promising lead, will a partner be able to assist you in selling the firm's services? Once you secure a new client, will you be rewarded for your efforts? Some firms will compensate associates up to one-third of all billable fees (minus expenses); other firms have a policy of not compensating associates for bringing in new clients but will count business development as a factor in partnership decisions and year-end raises.

If you know the profile of the ideal firm client and are interested in client development, now is a good time to begin cultivating clients and flexing your

➡ Why "Client-Getting Ability" Matters at Small Law Firms

The profit squeeze and income compression that has been a pattern for almost a decade is continuing. Some law firms have already taken steps to cope with these economic problems. For firms faced with decreasing profitability and an inability to compete well for top legal talent in a competitive and expensive environment, a more aggressive, proactive approach has become necessary to ensure long-term success and continuing profitability.

Many law firms today would agree with the above statement. However, what is particularly interesting about this statement is that it was written in 1989, not the year 2000. The above quote was written as the introduction to an article addressing a 15% increase nationally in associate salaries. Ah, for the good old days. And, if things couldn't get worse, today law firms find themselves confronting the challenges of six-figure starting associate salaries and a one-third associate turnover rate.

Why is it more critical at small firms than at large firms for associates to demonstrate marketing ability well before the time they are considered for partnership? The answers to this question, and many similar "partnership track" questions, are the same.

1. Law firms need to ensure a continual stream of new client work in order to survive as a business.

2. There is less depth in the ranks at small law firms. Therefore, each lawyer position in a small firm typically carries with it more management responsibility than in the large firm. "It's not enough anymore just to be a good lawyer."

The partnership track in small firms tends to be shorter than at large firms. Small law firms do not have the luxury that large law firms have of hiring many associates every year, secure in the knowledge that every year there usually will be a small group of promising associates to promote to partnership — if additional partners are even desired that year.

Large firm or small firm, one thing is true: a firm can't promote all of the associates to partner (shareholder, member, etc.).

The Florida Bar's Law Office Management Assistance Service recently conducted a study of trends in partnership criteria in small law firms. The study showed that the criteria used to evaluate associates for promotion to partnership are both subjective and objective. The results of this study were summarized into a "top ten list." The ability to obtain new business and market the firm's services was listed at number one and number four, respectively.

1. **Do we need any partners?** Will adding another partner enhance profitability, add depth to management, help to ensure the future of the firm, and bring business the firm wants?

2. **"You can't just sit in the back anymore."** Being "only" a brilliant lawyer is not good enough anymore. Only the largest firms can accommodate the "brilliant technician" in the partnership.

3. **Bad personalities need not apply.** Firms can no longer afford to tolerate 800-pound gorillas, lone rangers, abusive behavior — simply put, attorneys who refuse to be managed.

4. **Marketing skills.** The ability and willingness to work with a group to market the firm, and to predict economic trends and emerging client bases.

5. **Management skills.** The organizational skills necessary to manage a team assigned to complex legal matters, lead and manage a practice group, and participate in managing the firm.

6. **Quality of work product and work ethic.** Producing legal work of consistently superior quality and leading by example (work ethic).

7. **Leadership.** The ability and willingness to build consensus among the partnership. Will this lawyer cross-sell other departments? Does this person "have what it takes" to work within the partnership to bring its vision and goals to fruition?

8. **Profitability.** Caution: firms should be careful in analyzing associate numbers. Like paralegals, associates do not choose their assignments. On the other hand, has the associate demonstrated the ability to work efficiently alone and on teams to maximize case/matter profitability?

9. **Productivity.** Same caution as above. Do the numbers reflect consistency in productivity? Over the years, when work was slow, did the associate seek out assignments from partners? Do the other lawyers want this lawyer working on their matters?

10. **Peer evaluation and cultural fit.** What do the lawyers really think of this prospective partner? Typically, the smaller the firm, the more important are the results of peer evaluation.

Summary

The saying, "the more things change, the more they stay the same" was never more true than when law firm partners must determine what criteria will be used to evaluate and promote associates. The ability to obtain new business and market the firm's services will always be at the top, or near the top of the list.

The bottom-line question to law firm partners remains, "Do we want to be partners with this lawyer?" If yes, why? If not, why not? Each law firm must determine its own criteria for admitting new partners. Answering the preceding questions is a good start to developing satisfactory partnership criteria for the firm.

Judith D. Equels
The Florida Bar
Law Office Management Assistance Service

rainmaking muscles. By beginning your career with an eye toward client-getting, you increase the likelihood that you will find appropriate clients and persuade them to utilize your professional services.

There are some excellent books on client-getting. (The Appendix contains a list of resources.) In a nutshell, you should:

- ✓ Know your firm's areas of practice.
- ✓ Understand the firm's client profile and seek out appropriate matches for the firm's practice areas.
- ✓ Begin with the notion that you want to be active in the community and open to many possibilities of meeting people. Many times, clients appear in social settings: charitable activities, the barber shop, or the grocery store. Be alert to the potential for client-getting in different kinds of circumstances

and always display the highest degree of professionalism in all of your interactions.

✓ Remain positive in the face of competition. Bad-mouthing other lawyers in town demonstrates a lack of civility and engenders ill will. Potential clients should reach out to you on the basis of your professional skills and personality rather than your negativity.

✓ Take time to cultivate contacts. Often, clients need to get to know and trust you before they approach you with legal problems. Be patient with the client-getting process and cultivate your contacts by remembering them at holidays or other special life cycle events, clipping interesting articles that relate to their areas of interest, etc.

- **Client Relations**

Learning to attract business is only the beginning. In order to establish a successful small firm practice you need to engage in good client relations. Retain clients by being a good listener, responding to telephone calls within the hour, being accessible during work hours, and by being thoughtful and considerate. This means making periodic contact with clients to apprise them of the status of their cases either in writing, in person, or by telephone call.

Be sure to keep in touch with clients and to express an interest in their lives and their families. This is particularly the case with small firms where the personal touch is valued. Many lawyers make it a point to send holiday cards or small gifts to their clients. Periodic outings to sporting events, dinners

➡ Five Tips for Improving Your Client Relations

1. **Believe that the client is number one.** Attorneys need to take a customer service approach to dealing with clients. This may be a new concept for lawyers brought up on the idea of "client control," which basically means that the lawyer is the boss and the client better stay out of the way! Client control is an antiquated concept, and it has no place in the modern practice of law.

2. **Return phone calls.** Sounds simple, yet the single most frequently registered complaint with state bars across the country is the failure of attorneys to return their telephone calls. I know one attorney who has a very successful practice, and who keeps getting return clients. I asked him how he did it, and he let me in on his secret: he makes a point of returning all telephone calls within four hours.

3. **Visit the client.** You can learn a great deal about clients by visiting them in their place of business. A letter or a phone call can only go so far. In order to really understand clients, you need to learn about the territory where they live or work.

4. **Advise your clients about changes in the law that impact them.** When clients receive a note, clipping, or letter from you highlighting changes in the law that have occurred in your area of expertise, they will know that you're up to date and that you care about them. This is also a great marketing opportunity because, by sending clients information of related interest, you can let them know that you also perform services in these other areas.

5. **Communicate regularly with your clients.** It's important to let clients know what's happening with their matter, and one way to do that is to send status reports on a regular basis. Even if there is nothing much to report, tell the client that things are going as projected. Think of this communication as a way to educate the client about the legal process and as an opportunity for cementing your relationship.

Edward Poll, J.D., M.B.A., CMC, Los Angeles, California

or lunches, and theater tickets are common client relations tools. Never take clients for granted. Always take time to touch base and demonstrate thoughtfulness.

- **Ability to Work Independently**

Small firms are, by nature, thinly staffed operations. Typically, you will not find layers of entry-level, mid-level, and senior-level associates and paralegals assisting on a case. In fact, you may be the only lawyer working on a case. Accordingly, it is important for you to be able to work independently. This means undertaking an assignment and figuring out the answer without burdening the other lawyers with unnecessary questions or interruptions.

When you receive an assignment, listen carefully to the assigning attorney. Here are some guidelines when accepting assignments to help you work independently:

✓ Always listen carefully to the assigning attorney and ask questions at the end. Try not to interrupt the presentation midway through. Take notes to keep track of your thoughts and questions.

✓ If you understand the assignment, you may want to briefly repeat the stated task to ensure that you heard everything correctly. For example, "You want me to research the standard for summary judgment under Pennsylvania law and write a brief in support of summary judgment for the Rogers case by Tuesday using the three points you just mentioned. Is that right?"

✓ If you do not have the case file, ask where it can be found.

✓ Inquire if there are other resources that might be helpful in order for you to complete the assignment. If you are still a relatively new attorney, you may not be aware of some local resources that might ease your research.

✓ Ask whether or not it is proper for you to contact the client directly if you have any questions, or if questions should be filtered through the attorney.

✓ If you think that using a subscription database such as LexisNexis® or Westlaw® would ease your research, ask before logging on. At some firms, particularly small firms, LexisNexis® and Westlaw® research can be expensive or particular clients might refuse to pay for those services. Some partners may ask to see your query before you log on. A good rule is to ask first, log on later.

✓ Learn if there are billable hours requirements for the assignment and stick to them. Some assigning attorneys will say: "This should not take more than ten hours." Keep tabs on your time. Should you reach a roadblock or discover that additional research is required, keep the assigning attorney apprised of ongoing developments so she or he is not surprised to discover excessive time.

✓ Know the deadline for completing the assignment and stick to it. If you get lost in the weeds with a deadline approaching, inform the assigning attorney as early as possible. Often, missed deadlines are not only client relations nightmares but also risk actual malpractice liability if filing dates are missed and statutes of limitations expire.

● Interpersonal Skills

Interpersonal skills can be summed up as the ability to conform, to get along in social and work situations, to empathize with the feelings of others, and to treat others with respect. Intelligence, while an important factor in career success, is part of a much larger scheme. During my tenure as director of career services, I witnessed too many academically gifted students stumble and fall in the job search process due to poor interpersonal skills. A lack of interpersonal skills can strike a fatal blow to long-term success.

Examine your interpersonal skills and make an effort to conform to the work environment in which you find yourself. Conformity does not mean forcing yourself to fit a cookie-cutter mold. Effective lawyers encompass a range of different styles and orientations. These differences should be recognized and appreciated because clients do not come in a "one-size-fits-all" pattern. Nonetheless, certain proprieties ought to be observed in order to succeed in the workplace. These include appropriate dress and grooming at all times, showing up for work on a regular basis and explaining absences well in advance, good communication skills, and respect for all individuals in the workplace, especially support staff. Take a look around your workplace and note how lawyers dress, when they arrive for work and when they depart, and how people communicate with one another. Make an effort to model the best behavior of the more experienced attorneys.

Treat your secretary and all support staff with the utmost respect. Not only will you impart dignity to the work environment, but you will also develop very

➡ Developing and Managing Associates in the Smaller Law Firm: An Ideal System

A smaller law firm needs to develop and implement a game plan that identifies its objectives for recruiting and hiring one or more associates. At the beginning of their careers, associates need: (1) direction and supervision in performing client work; (2) information about the firm's plans and procedures, particularly the aspects that affect their work; (3) feedback on their performance; and (4) information about how they rate and if they fit into the firm's future plans.

A law firm should develop and implement a plan for monitoring the progress and performance of associates and evaluate the results in light of the firm's objectives. This oversight function should be performed and coordinated by a designated partner or committee of partners. This individual or committee should be accountable to the partners for coordinating the associate recruiting, career development, and communication program. The "professional personnel partner" should be responsible for providing information to associates on firm matters relating to development and career opportunities and for administering associate evaluations.

Formal or informal associates' meetings should be held monthly, every other month, or quarterly to cover the basic aspects of client matters, administrative matters, workload, assignments, and training programs; future plans, logistics of handling various types of cases; billings and collections; firm policy; public relations and marketing opportunities; unusual situations; professional responsibility and ethics; and general developments in the profession.

One of the best methods of managing associates is to set up a system whereby an associate works closely with a few partners yet is paired with a single partner who also serves as a mentor. In this system, the mentor should meet with the associate regularly to review his or her workload, problems, and potential conflicts. Each assigned client matter should have a recommended due date, and the partner assigning the work should make sure the associate has a thorough understanding of the issues involved. In many firms, associates communicate with their mentor, verbally or in writing, about their workload and availability. They may be requested to account for the next 14 work days by estimating availability, and the number of billable hours to be recorded, for the following two-week intervals. This will enable the mentor to have a summary of the associates' current and projected workloads.

Objective information about each associate should be compiled and reviewed to determine how well they are doing in producing their targeted number of billable hours. Write-offs and write-downs of associate time should also be analyzed by the responsible attorney on a monthly basis to determine the reasons for such action. If any associate falls short of the estimated hours, the professional personnel partner should discuss the matter with the individual on an informal basis. Thus, if a partner is writing off too much time, or an associate is not recording enough hours, the firm will be able to remedy the situation at an early and critical stage. It will be able to step in and protect its leverage by making certain the associates are gainfully employed, adequately supervised, and assigned enough profitable work to allow them to achieve their targets. The information provided in these reports and the professional personnel partner's experience in working closely with the associates, will enable him or her to make recommendations on the associates' salary progression.

Meetings about time-keeping issues should not take the place of formal evaluations. A formal associate evaluation should be conducted at six-month intervals for the first 18 months an associate is employed by the firm, and annually thereafter until the associate becomes a member of the firm. The partners should plan to conduct a formal, one-on-one, evaluation with all associates, utilizing a written evaluation form as the basis for these meetings.

If the firm neglects to utilize the information that is readily available through the associates' evaluation program, it is undermining its own potential profitability. This is the point at which to begin to build incentives into the system to encourage exemplary performance. This is the occasion for reward or remedy, as the evaluation results warrant. The point of the monitoring process is to arm the firm with tools that will enable it to formulate plans to meet its staffing requirements.

The partners must be willing to make an investment in the future by becoming more involved in the associates' early experience at the firm. By monitoring each associate's progress, under the auspices of the professional personnel partner and the individual partner-mentors, the firm can build toward its future.

Joel A. Rose, President
Joel A. Rose & Associates, Inc.
Management Consultants to Law Offices
Cherry Hill, New Jersey

powerful allies to help you in the early years of your career. I still recall my first secretary in private practice, who used to remind me to sign my pleadings before sending them to be filed. Had I not fostered a good relationship with my secretary, she could have burned me by letting the pleading get to the court clerk without my signature and blowing the statute of limitations for our client.

Poor interpersonal skills within the office will sink an otherwise promising career as surely as they will in the larger world. Make every effort to foster good people skills. For example:

- ✓ **Never, ever yell at support staff.** Even if the other lawyers at the firm are screamers, resist the temptation to yell when stress levels rise. You demean yourself and others by losing control. Plus, you create an environment of blame where others focus on damage control rather than results.

- ✓ **Give instructions clearly and answer questions.** Secretaries and receptionists want to feel a part of the workplace and, by explaining the work, you help them to feel that they are part of a team. Do not assume that secretaries are dumb. To the contrary, many of the best secretaries are bright and interested in learning more. They have simply made a different career choice. Not everyone wants to be a lawyer!

- ✓ **Reward support staff with kind words.** Say "thank you" for a job well done. Be sure to let others know that you are pleased with their work. Deliver criticism behind closed doors.

✓ **Remember birthdays, anniversaries, and Secretary's Day.** Recognize special events.

● **Partnership**

Partnership means an ownership interest in the firm. Whereas an associate is an employee of the firm, a partner generally owns part (or all) of the business. This means that a partner shares in the overall financial success of the business during good times and shoulders the burden of an economic downtime. While partnership often confers a degree of tenure, the fact remains that partnership requires tenacity, client building, and a strong record for successful representation and retention of clients. While the financial upside of partnership is obvious at a successful small firm, when business is slow you cannot count on a regular paycheck.

The partnership track will vary from firm to firm. Larger firms tend to utilize a lock-step approach to partnership decisions: for example, after eight years, an associate at a large firm may be eligible to be considered for partnership and may have two chances to be voted in by a majority of the owners. At smaller firms, fewer rules exist to guide associates regarding partnership decisions. At some small firms, partners can be named quite early (less than five years), while at other firms associates will wait more than ten years. If you are working at a family-owned firm, you may never be considered for partnership. As one hiring partner at a small firm explained, "When the time is right, we will name partners. There are no hard and fast rules."

Ideally, discussions about partnership possibilities should take place during the interview process or during the first year. You should know your firm's timeline for partnership and understand the ground rules. In general, some of the basic criteria for partnership at any firm include: demonstrated competency to practice law, client-getting skills, loyalty to the firm, and interpersonal skills. Of course, different firms will stress different aspects of the aforementioned guideposts, and you should know how your firm values and weights the various prerequisites for partnership.

Some firms will offer different partnership options. The traditional partnership arrangement is known as a "full partnership equity interest," where a partner becomes an owner of the business and receives his or her compensation based more or less directly upon the overall success of the firm. Compensation is typically based upon client-getting skills. Therefore, the partner with the most lucrative clients might be compensated more highly than a partner with less successful client-getting skills. This arrangement is sometimes referred to as the "eat what you kill" model of compensation. At other firms, partner compensation is based upon other factors such as seniority. Still other firms have a "non-equity partnership interest," in which some partners may technically be "owners" but are compensated on a fixed-salary basis, without bearing the risk — or reaping the reward — of fluctuations in the firm's profits from year to year.

Becoming a partner is a tremendous professional accomplishment. At the same time, it creates new and different stressors in your life. Some students imagine partnership as the pinnacle of professional success. While partnership may signal a level of professional competency, it also creates new demands on your time. Not only must you find and retain paying clients, you may also need to take part in the running of the business, including hiring, firing, and public relations.

Overcoming Roadblocks to Success

After a long and sometimes difficult job search, many students dream that, once they receive their law degrees and pass the bar exam, professional success is all but assured. Unfortunately, success is never certain and you need to remain vigilant about your continuing career goals. Throughout your career you will encounter roadblocks and deadends as you strive for professional and personal success. Vaulting over the roadblocks that you will inevitably encounter and learning from your mistakes is the secret to any career success.

Hiring partners and practitioners cite the number one reason that young lawyers fail to succeed at a law firm as being failed expectations. Make sure that you understand clearly your firm's expectations, as well as your own, and then dedicate yourself to meeting and surpassing those expectations.

➡ The Importance of Bar Associations to the Small Firm Practitioner

Small firm practitioners often utilize their membership in a local bar association as a résumé enhancer, without thinking more practically about how the membership can enhance their overall practice. Membership in a bar association is a cost-effective way for attorneys to network with and market their practice to their peers; obtain a discount on mandatory continuing education course fees; and, in those associations with their own libraries, use a free resource center for legal treatises and research assistance. Additionally, many bar associations now provide services specifically tailored to the solo and small firm practitioner, such as law practice management and career guidance and mentoring programs.

In order to make the most of a membership in a bar association, an attorney needs to do more than send in his or her annual dues. An attorney should join a committee at the bar association or volunteer his or her time at *pro bono* programs sponsored by the bar association, preferably in a committee or *pro bono* program in which the attorney would like to spend time. By engaging in an enjoyable and worthwhile activity, the attorney will more likely remain involved. It is from an ongoing commitment that an attorney meets and gets to know peers, developing relationships that may eventually result in friendships, referrals, and informal mentoring.

For the sole practitioner, a bar association provides respite from the isolation that often can occur, especially for those who may be practicing out of their homes. When a bar association provides services that bring solo practitioners together to share and compare law practice management techniques, the camaraderie and information obtained can be invaluable. Many bar associations have law practice management sections or committees that provide information and guidance on the business of the practice of law.

Because the cost of maintaining a full service library is beyond the means of most small firm practitioners, membership in a bar association can provide considerable cost savings on research. If a bar association has its own library, an attorney can obtain free access to legal treatises, cases and statutes, and, sometimes, copies of legal memoranda and appellate briefs and other useful forms. The library staff can assist in reducing the amount of time spent by the attorney looking for the right research source for a project. For the bar associations without libraries, many offer as a member benefit, reduced rates for subscriptions to Westlaw® or LexisNexis®.

Membership in a bar association can provide small firm practitioners with many tangible benefits and is well worth the cost of the annual dues when fully utilized by practitioners.

Lisa M. Bluestein
Director, Small Law Firm Center
Association of the Bar of the City of New York

CHAPTER 5:

Life After the Small Law Firm

"The way to success: First, have a clear goal, not a fuzzy one."

NORMAN VINCENT PEALE

Is there life after a small firm? The answer is a re-sounding "yes!" This chapter will discuss career options within and outside the legal profession after your first small firm work experience, how to position yourself for the inevitable moves that are now part of the legal profession, and how to find the right life work for you.

Over the last twenty years, the legal profession has become more mobile, as lawyers change jobs with greater frequency than ever before. Previously, one often graduated from law school, chose an employer, and remained with that employer for one's entire career. That trend has reversed in recent years. Within the first two years of practice, nearly a quarter of the associates at law firms of all sizes have moved on, according to the NALP Foundation report entitled *Keeping the Keepers II: Mobility and Management of Associates*. After nearly five years, more than half of those hired out of law school have left their original firms. While the five-year attrition rate for women (54.9%) was only slightly higher for men (52.3%), the attrition rates for minority lawyers was significantly higher. The five-year attrition rate for minority male lawyers was 68% and the attrition rate for female minority lawyers was 64.4%.

Changing employers is a natural consequence of professional development these days. In fact, staying put and not exploring different opportunities at regular intervals during your career may work to your detriment by foreclosing new options.

Moving on after a small law firm requires careful consideration. Simply moving around in hopes of finding the right place for you is rarely a successful strategy. Ask yourself, "Why do I want to leave this firm? What am I seeking?" Some lawyers leave for higher salaries or improved partnership opportunities. Others move in order to shift to a different practice area or geographic location. After working at a small firm, some lawyers realize that they want to pursue a nontraditional career or hang their own shingle and practice solo.

Whether or not you are contemplating a move right now or in the near future, staying current with changes in the legal marketplace is important. Read about professional developments within your local bar association and keep in touch with law school classmates and colleagues. If you receive calls from a professional recruiter about lateral opportunities, listen politely even if you are not interested. While you may not be ready to make a move this year, you may change your mind the following year and a professional recruiter can be a valuable asset in the lateral job market. Maltreating a professional recruiter who is making preliminary

➡ Life After Small Firm Practice

Following four years of working at a well-respected small law firm in Pittsburgh, I decided to work on a business I had started in my second year at the firm. What I like about this decision is that my business revolves around placing temporary attorneys at firms and companies in the region. I have found I have learned much more about the practice of law in this capacity than I did working hard on narrow, discrete projects.

The other aspect is that I am pleased to have something of a life. Law at the associate level involves solving complex problems that oftentimes have no solution. Cerebrally it is challenging and very tiring. Even when you have some free time as an attorney, you are invariably brain dead after work. Law to me also seemed to put blinders on me to life and other interests because building a successful legal career requires so much focus and time commitment. Today as a business owner I still work hard. However, my business revolves around working with people, and the fatigue is less mind draining. Having said that, I do miss the camaraderie of a law firm. There is something special about putting a number of very intelligent people together and having them work hard on projects together. An almost boot-camp bonding happens in a law firm that is unmatched in selling professions or other business functions.

I am glad I did work as an attorney at a small firm and sometimes I miss it. But I am more pleased with my decision to take a chance and focus on my business. Therefore, it is important to realize there are other things you can do with your life than practice law.

Karl A. Schieneman, Esq.
Managing Director, Legal Network Ltd.
Pittsburgh, PA

inquiries is a sure-fire way to burn bridges that might help you in the future.

Before making a move, contemplate your rationale for leaving and begin gathering information with your ultimate goal in mind. Here are just a few of the traditional routes that lawyers take following their first small firm stint.

Switching to Another Small Firm

If you already have full-time experience at a small firm, then it is a fairly straightforward matter to express an interest in another small firm. Some common reasons for switching to another small firm are a desire to move into a different practice area or geographic region, to raise your visibility with a more prominent firm, to earn more money, or to increase your chances at partnership. Any or all of the aforementioned reasons are valid reasons to consider making a change.

Since small firms are all different, exercise your due diligence skills and learn about the character and quality of the firms to which you seek to apply. Talk to fellow practitioners about the reputation of the firm, the partners, staffing issues, compensation, and any other issues that concern you.

To find opportunities at other small firms, consider the following resources:

✓ Local bar association publications and websites.

✓ Networking.

✓ A professional recruiter/search consultant.

✓ Independent research, including research through Internet sites.

✓ Your law school career services office alumni publication.

Approach small firm opportunities with a cover letter and résumé, unless requested otherwise. Request in your cover letter that your inquiry remain confidential; however, realize — particularly in small legal communities and within specialty practice areas — that colleagues speak to one another and your job search may not remain secret for long.

Moving to a Larger Firm

Years ago, it would have been hard for a small firm associate to market herself or himself to a large firm. The wisdom of bygone years was: "it's easier to move from a large firm to a smaller firm than vice versa." That is not necessarily the case today. There appears to be greater fluidity in the legal marketplace and larger firms recognize that small firms offer associates excellent training and experience that often transfers to a larger firm environment. Larger firms will still express an interest in your academic achievements during law school, but grades may begin to pale in comparison to relevant work experience.

In most cases, a larger firm will be able to offer higher compensation and a greater range of benefits. In addition, larger firms tend to have more developed administrative infrastructures that allow their lawyers to staff cases with more people. As with any contemplated move, gather information and learn about the firm — its practice areas, its reputation in the community, partnership possibilities, and related areas of concern for you individually.

Since partnership decisions at larger firms typically begin around the seventh year, you ought to consider trying to switch to a larger firm after no more than five years at a small firm if partnership is your ultimate goal. The primary reason for making a move by your fifth year is that you will need to prove your client-getting mettle and demonstrate your proficiency as a lawyer in order to be considered for partnership at a larger firm. If business development is not your forte, or if you are otherwise not pursuing an equity partnership position, larger firms might offer you an of counsel position or, depending on the partnership structure, a salaried partner position. Both of counsel and the salaried partner positions recognize experience but do not tie compensation to client-getting skills.

If you are already a partner at a small firm, one of the defining issues confronting your marketability at a larger firm will be the number of clients you can bring with you to your new firm, the profitability of your book of business, and your potential for business development.

To find opportunities with larger firms, consider the following resources:

✓ National and local bar association publications.

✓ Networking/word-of-mouth.

✓ A professional recruiter/search consultant.

✓ Independent research, including Internet research.

✓ Your law school career services office alumni publication.

Seeking Assistance: What Is a Legal Search Consultant and When Should You Call One?

A legal search consultant (sometimes known in the vernacular as a "headhunter") helps law firms and other organizations to identify and hire individuals whose credentials match the needs of the employer. A legal search consultant is paid by the organization seeking to make the hire. Fees for placement vary, but it is not unusual for a search consultant to receive a fee equaling one-quarter or more of the starting salary. So, if your starting salary is $100,000, then the search consultant who facilitated the successful placement would be paid $25,000 directly by the firm. You would receive your regular salary regardless of the fee paid to the professional recruiter. *Beware of legal search consultants or placement agencies who offer to assist you in exchange for a fee that you pay up front.*

Legal search consultants do not typically deal with recent graduates who have not passed the bar examination, although this may vary depending on your locale. In most cases, professional recruiters find experienced, licensed professionals with particular skills needed by an employer. A lawyer with prior full-time work experience is called a lateral hire. Since fresh graduates who are awaiting bar results typically do not have expertise in a particular practice area, it is unlikely that a legal search consultant would help you in your initial job search. However, once you have passed the bar and gained some practice experience, approaching a consultant and presenting your credentials might be a worthwhile move.

To learn more about legal search consultants in your area, contact your law school career services office or check out the *Legal Recruiters Directory* published annually by *The American Lawyer*.

Working for a Government Agency

Did you know that the federal government is the single largest employer of lawyers in this country? The Department of Justice alone employs more than 9,000 lawyers (*Federal Government Agencies Which Employ Attorneys*, compiled by the Office of Attorney Personnel Management, U.S. Department of Justice). Working for a federal, state, or local government agency can be an ideal place for a lawyer with prior experience at a smaller firm.

Lawyers engaged in government practice express a higher degree of satisfaction in their work lives than do their private firm counterparts. This is due, in part, to more manageable work hours, a shared public service mission, and a strong sense of camaraderie. Government lawyers can also exercise a considerable amount of professional power. A lawyer with the Food and Drug Administration, for example, is empowered to close down a food manufacturing company that is operating out of compliance with federal statutes.

Salaries for federal attorneys are based on a matrix of grades and steps formulated by the federal government. The salary for most entry-level federal attorney positions is set at the GS-11, Step-1 level ($44,136 at the time this book was revised). Adjustments for prior experience, locale, cost of living, or additional graduate degrees will vary based on individual cases.

To focus yourself on finding a government agency position, consider both your geographic constraints and your areas of expertise. For example, if you have experience in labor and employment law, it makes sense to explore opportunities with entities such as the Department of Labor, the Office of Administrative Law Judges (ALJ), and the federal, state, or local equivalents of the Equal Employment Opportunity Commission. Likewise, if your interests lie in the field of environmental law, focus on the federal, state, and local versions of the Environmental Protection Agency.

Government-related work also includes positions in U.S. Attorney's offices and Public Defender's offices. Some states contract out public defender work to private public interest organizations, and some public defender offices are structured as separate entities. If this type of work appeals to you, research how offices are structured and how hiring takes place in your area.

Be prepared for a slow and protracted job search when seeking a government position. Unlike private firms that tend to make quick decisions, government agencies may take months to make a hiring decision.

You may have to complete detailed forms (such as the SF-161), and provide information to commence a security clearance. Your résumé will differ from a typical private firm résumé and should list information such as date of birth, Social Security number and other personal data that is traditionally left off a résumé created for the private sector. With government hiring, patience is a virtue and your reward will be a legal career that many on the inside describe as professionally fulfilling and as often providing a higher quality-of-life quotient (i.e., a better work/life balance) than those in private practice.

If you are an experienced attorney, be aware that government agencies may have different procedures for lateral hiring than for entry-level hires. For example, while entry-level hiring at the Department of Justice is centralized, lateral hiring is carried out by the Department's separate divisions.

To find opportunities with federal and state agencies, consider the following resources:

✓ National, local, and specialty bar association publications.

✓ Networking.

✓ Independent research, including Internet research. For a detailed list of federal government resources on the Internet, see page 152.

✓ Equal Justice Works (*www.equaljusticeworks.org*), formerly the National Association for Public Interest Law (NAPIL), leads the country in organizing, training, and supporting public service-minded law students and in creating summer and postgraduate public interest jobs. Each October, Equal Justice Works holds a job fair and education conference in Washington, D.C. featuring public interest employers, including government agencies. Recent law graduates may attend this event. The job fair employer list is usually posted on their website in early September.

✓ PSLawNet (*www.pslawnet.org*), NALP's Public Service Law Network Worldwide, is a network of approximately 150 law schools. PSLawNet offers a database of over 12,000 public interest and government agencies in the U.S. and around the world. Users can perform customized searches of public interest and government opportunities around the

➡️ ## Tapping into State and Local Bar Associations in Texas

Seventy-six percent of Texas lawyers in private practice work in firms of 24 or fewer attorneys. The Law Office Management Program (*www.texasbar.com/lomp*) was implemented by the State Bar of Texas to establish processes and procedures to assist solo and small firm practitioners in the delivery of legal services through efficient and effective law office management practices. Many state and local bar associations play a leading role in assisting solo and small firm practitioners.

Gisela B. Bradley, Director
The Law Office Management Program
The State Bar of Texas
Austin, TX

world, ranging from short-term volunteer and paid internships to full-time jobs, fellowships, and *pro bono* opportunities.

✓ Your law school career services office alumni publication.

Pursuing Public Interest Work

After practicing with a small firm, some lawyers choose to pursue careers with public interest organizations. These include not only legal services organizations but also a wide variety of other public interest organizations, such as those that lobby in specific public interest areas. While public interest practice generally is not as lucrative as private practice, lawyers serving the public interest tend to be immensely satisfied and enjoy a sense of camaraderie that many of their private sector peers lack. National employment statistics indicate that only about 3% of all law school graduates obtain public interest employment directly following graduation (although, when government employment and judicial clerkships are included, about 25% obtain public sector employment). High student debt loads may be one factor discouraging the selection of public interest employment, but it is also true that public interest organizations tend to have small legal staffs and, therefore, to value lawyers who can hit the ground running. You will find that access to public interest opportunities increases once you gain some lateral experience elsewhere.

In directing résumés to public interest organizations, keep in mind that one of the key factors informing hiring decisions is prior experience in public interest law or in community service activities. Thus, when directing a résumé to a public interest organization, stress *pro bono* work, prior public interest experience while in law school, prior and current community service work, and organizations that demonstrate a commitment to social justice issues.

To find opportunities with public interest organizations, consider the following resources:

- ✓ National, state, local, and specialty bar association publications.
- ✓ Networking.
- ✓ Equal Justice Works (*www.equaljusticeworks.org*), formerly the National Association for Public Interest Law (NAPIL), leads the country in organizing, training, and supporting public service-minded law students and in creating summer and postgraduate public interest jobs. Each October, Equal Justice Works holds a job fair and education conference in Washington, D.C. featuring public interest employers, including government agencies. Recent law graduates may attend this event. The job fair employer list is usually posted on their web site in early September.
- ✓ PSLawNet (*www.pslawnet.org*), NALP's Public Service Law Network Worldwide, is a network of approximately 150 law schools. PSLawNet offers a database of over 12,000 public interest and government agencies in the U.S. and around the

world. Users can perform customized searches of public interest and government opportunities around the world, ranging from short-term volunteer and paid internships to full-time jobs, fellowships, and *pro bono* opportunities.

✓ For a compilation of private firms engaged in public interest legal matters, read *Private Public Interest and Plaintiff's Firm Guide*, a joint project of the Center for Public Interest Law at Columbia Law School and the Bernard Koteen Office of Public Interest Advising at Harvard Law School (2004).

✓ Your law school career services office alumni publication.

Starting a Solo Practice

After learning the ropes at a small firm, some lawyers become solo practitioners and run their own businesses. Solo practice, whether on a full- or part-time basis, requires careful consideration and preparation as well as a detailed business plan. You need to consider issues, such as:

✓ Your areas of practice.

✓ Your ideal (or your real) client base.

✓ Advertising and public relations.

✓ Malpractice and liability insurance.

✓ Support staff, if any.

✓ Office location.

✓ Print and online research materials.

➡ Life as a Solo Practitioner

As a solo practitioner with a J.D. and M.B.A., solo practice fits my lifestyle and allows me to spend more time with my family. I may be at the office at 2 a.m. sometimes, but I can also be home at 3 p.m., if necessary. I also enjoy the intellectual freedom my practice provides. I decide how to handle a matter or whether to take a matter at all. I do not have to do the work I do not want to do. Having practiced with a small firm before opening my own solo practice, I think the biggest initial downside of small firm practice is money. You most likely will make more in a large firm, and the income will be consistent. As a solo practitioner, the money in the early stages of your firm is either very good or very bad. My solo practice is in its third year and the money is finally beginning to be more consistent. I still at this time make less than I could in a large firm, however many small firm practitioners with well-established practices make more than attorneys in large firms. Another downside is mentoring and training: generally speaking, larger firms may have much better systems for this (of course, in a large firm you may not try a case for years, whereas in a small firm you likely will). Small firms will hire when the workload requires more people; generally speaking, they cannot hire every year like a large firm. Many small firms consider work experience, working through school, and substantive activities such as moot court and mock trial. Small firms often focus less on grades as compared to large firms.

Donald E. Teller, Jr.
Law Office of Donald E. Teller, Jr., P.C.
Colleyville, Texas

An excellent book to read before delving into solo practice is *How to Start and Build a Law Practice* by Jay G. Foonberg (American Bar Association, 5th Edition, 2004). Foonberg provides in-depth information about starting one's own practice, from choosing a location to selecting malpractice insurance to getting clients. For other resources on solo practice and related matters, see the Appendix on page 158.

Obtaining a Judicial Clerkship

Judicial clerkships used to be filled with recent law graduates interested in working with an experienced jurist who would teach them to become more proficient researchers and writers. Typically, a judicial clerkship would last either one or two years and conclude with the law clerk moving into a full-time position in private practice, government, or public interest law.

This pattern has shifted in recent years. Nowadays, some judges on both the federal and state levels are interested in hiring experienced lawyers to handle research, analysis, and writing duties on either a short-term or long-term basis. The reason for this shift can be attributed to several, non-related factors: (1) some judges prefer to create an ongoing professional rapport with a trusted employee rather than hiring someone new every year or two; (2) some judges have made nonproductive hires and seek to avoid that dilemma in the future by hiring a permanent law clerk whom the judge knows well; and (3) lawyers themselves are opting out of traditional practice options and are seeking out permanent affiliations with judges because they enjoy the work as well as the flexibility that typically comes with a judicial clerkship experience.

The primary responsibilities of a judicial clerk entail research, analysis, and drafting. If you enjoy carefully poring over voluminous documents, researching obscure areas of law, and working in a very quiet, sometimes solitary, environment, then clerking on either a permanent or a temporary basis could be a great job for you.

Law clerks on the federal level typically begin at GS-11, Step 1 ($44,136 at the time of publication) with adjustments made for cost of living, prior relevant work experience, and additional graduate degrees. While you will not make as much as you would in private practice, law clerks enjoy very satisfying work lives (so long as they get along with their bosses).

Some judges seeking to fill law clerk positions will turn to their former clerks or summer interns. With that in mind, it might be helpful to keep in touch with your former judicial employers and keep them apprised of your progress. Should a permanent clerkship position become available, you will be in a favorable position.

For a full listing of judicial clerkship resources, see the Appendix on page 153.

Embarking on a Nontraditional Career

You may decide that practicing law in the traditional sense is not a fulfilling career path. Whether you tire of the hours and the professional demands, or simply do not find satisfaction in the day-to-day challenges of practice, deciding to shift your talents elsewhere can be both liberating and frightening. Should you decide to pursue a nontraditional career, take the time to plan carefully. A hastily made decision to leave the profession is never a good long-term strategy.

Good news: a law degree is one of the most transferable graduate degrees. The chief trait of any lawyer is the ability to solve problems — that is, to take a complex issue, break it down into logical components, find innovative solutions, and communicate those concepts to an unknowing audience.

Creative analytical and problem-solving skills are transferable to nearly any endeavor. The trick is finding the right career path for you. Gina Sauer, former Assistant Dean of Career Services at William Mitchell College of Law in St. Paul, Minnesota, formulated this equation for nontraditional career aspirants:

J.D. degree + _____ = Nontraditional Career

The trick, of course, is filling in the blank. Often, students and graduates have some vague ideas about potential nontraditional career paths but no definitive plans. Some have no idea where to begin; others expect the right job to appear spontaneously.

First, you need to decide how best to fill in the blank in the preceding equation. In addition to your J.D. degree, what are your talents and strengths? For example, law graduates with a strong interest in finance issues might find that financial planning or investment advising positions are an ideal use of their skills and talents.

The possibilities are endless when you begin to explore your interests as they relate to the world outside law. Your greatest challenge will be discerning how your J.D. degree connects with your ultimate career goals and approaching potential nontraditional employers with confidence. Two excellent resources to consult as you consider nontraditional options are *What Can You Do with a Law Degree?* by Deborah Arron (DecisionBooks, 2003) and *The Lawyer's Career Change Handbook* by Hindi Greenberg (HarperCollins, 1998).

Marketing Yourself

One of the greatest roadblocks to a nontraditional career is convincing an employer that you are right for the job. The key to any career move, whether within or outside the legal profession, is effective marketing of your skills and experience. The biggest mistake that students and graduates make in conducting their job searches is assuming that good things will happen to them simply because they have earned a law degree. "My résumé speaks for itself" is a common refrain from law students who believe that self-promotion is déclassé. Wrong! The best way to distinguish yourself in a competitive market is to promote yourself, your specific skills, and your experience as it relates to your desired outcome.

Begin your marketing campaign by considering your strengths and achievements. Create a list of your strong points as a worker. Ask yourself if you excel at any of the following skills:

_____ Writing briefs, contracts, or other legal documents

_____ Legal research

_____ Analysis

_____ Oral communication skills

_____ Client-getting/rainmaking

_____ Client relations

_____ Meeting deadlines

_____ Thinking creatively

_____ Leadership skills

_____ Organizational management

_____ Interpersonal skills

_____ Other (list): _____

Talk to friends and family as well as objective observers and ask them to comment on your strengths and achievements. Sometimes, we tend to discount our strengths and focus unduly on our failings. Let others reflect back to you what they perceive so that you can fully inventory your strengths as well as your weaknesses.

Seeking the help of professional career counselors can be helpful. If you are still in law school, visit your career services office. As a graduate, you may still have access to your career services office and its resources.

Your local bar association may offer confidential career counseling and networking opportunities. Use all of the resources at your disposal to help you make an intelligent career change.

Consider taking the Myers-Briggs Type Indicator instrument (MBTI) to assess your strengths and weaknesses. The MBTI is a detailed test to measure psychological type in order to help counsel individuals regarding a range of matters, including career choices. There are several excellent books that use the MBTI as a point of departure for discussing career goals, including *Do What You Are*, by Paul D. Tieger and Barbara Barron-Tieger (Little, Brown and Company, 2001). In order to take the Myers-Briggs Type Indicator, you need to visit a career counselor, psychologist, or social worker trained in this evaluation technique. If you are a law student and your school offers professional counseling, you may be able to take the MBTI and receive professional feedback without charge. This is a tremendous opportunity, and I encourage you to pursue this while you are still a student, since professional counseling services can cost hundreds of dollars.

Once you know where your strengths and professional interests lie, advertise and exploit your talents. For those of you who were raised with the admonition to avoid bragging at all costs, I give you permission to ignore that rule. A 10-year-old braggart is not the same as a law school graduate exploring a career shift. Hiding your talents or demanding that others discern your strengths for you could be the difference between a job offer and a polite "thanks, but no thanks."

If you are uncomfortable with the self-promotion aspect of the job search, rehearse and become comfortable saying positive things about yourself such as: "I enjoy litigating and successfully argued before Judge Jones on a recent case involving an appeal from the arbitration division. I won the argument and the client was very pleased with the result."

Whether you choose to practice law or decide that a nontraditional career suits you better, keep in mind that your legal training — the demanding research, writing, and analytical skills you acquired and honed — will serve you well in nearly any capacity. Small firm practice, with its emphasis on client service, serves as an excellent proving ground for other pursuits. So, choose small and be smart about all the career options on the horizon.

APPENDIX:

Resources (by Subject)

Clothes and Grooming

Beyond Casual Dress: What to Wear to Work If You Want to Get Ahead by Ann Marie Sabath (Career Press, 2000). The author, who runs At Ease Inc., which provides business protocol and etiquette workshops nationwide, discusses appropriate business attire.

The New Professional Image: From Business Casual to the Ultimate Power Look by Susan Bixler and Nancy Nix-Rice (Adams Media Corporation, 1997). Susan Bixler, a top corporate image consultant, addresses appropriate or effective dress in a "business casual" environment.

Work Clothes: Casual Dress for Serious Work by Kim Johnson Gross and Jeff Stone (Knopf, 1996). Part of the "Chic Simple" series, this photographic guide helps demonstrate how to put together a casual dress wardrobe piece by piece.

Casual Power: How to Power Up Your Nonverbal Communication & Dress Down for Success by Sherry Maysonave (Bright Books Inc., 1999). The author, founder and president of Empowerment Enterprises, discusses nonverbal communication skills, particularly casual attire and its impact on your image.

What to Wear: A Style Handbook by Kimberly Bonnell (St. Martin's Press, 1999). The former Fashion Director of *Glamour Magazine* writes about casual dress in the workplace.

Cover Letters

Sample cover letters follow beginning on page 162.

Guerrilla Tactics for Getting the Legal Job of Your Dreams by Kimm Alayne Walton (Harcourt/BarBri, 1999). Chapter 5 deals with cover letters directed to legal employers.

The following books discuss general cover letter dos and don'ts:

Cover Letter Magic by Wendy S. Enelow and Louise Kursmark (JIST Works, 2000).

The Everything Cover Letter Book by Steven Graber and Mark Lipsman (Adams Business Media, 2000).

The Guide to Basic Cover Letter Writing by Steven A. Provenzano (McGraw-Hill, 1994).

The Perfect Cover Letter (3rd Edition) by Richard H. Beatty (John Wiley & Sons, 2003).

7-Minute Cover Letters: Build the Perfect Cover Letter One 7-Minute Lesson at a Time by Dana Morgan (Arco Publications, 2000).

Interview Skills

An Insider's Guide to Interviewing: Insights from the Employer's Perspective (NALP booklet, 2002). Order from NALP's online bookstore at *www.nalp.org*.

Conquer Interview Objections by Robert F. Wilson and Erik H. Rambusch (John Wiley & Sons, 1994).

The Interview Rehearsal Book: 7 Steps to Job-Winning Interviews Using Acting Skills You Never Knew You Had by Deb Gottesman and Buzz Mauro (Berkley Publishing Group, 1999).

Power Interviews: Job-Winning Tactics From Fortune 500 Recruiters (revised and expanded edition) by Neil M. Yaeger and Lee Hough (John Wiley & Sons, 1998).

Sweaty Palms: The Neglected Art of Being Interviewed by H. Anthony Medley (Ten Speed Press, 1992).

Government Resources

Washington Information Directory (Congressional Quarterly, Inc., annual editions). An in-depth resource containing information about government and nonprofit organizations.

Federal Legal Employment Opportunities Guide, updated annually and provided as a downloadable file on NALP's website, *www.nalp.org*.

The following websites contain federal job listings:

Office of Personnel Management (OPM) USA-JOBS Web page — *http://usajobs.opm.gov*

U.S. Department of State Recruitment Web page — *http://www.state.gov/www/careers/index.html*

America's Job Bank — *http://ajb.dni.us*

Federal Jobs Digest — *http://www.jobsfed.com*

FedWorld Information Network — *http://www.fedworld.gov/*

The LSU U.S. Federal Government Agencies page — *http://www.lib/lsu.edu/gov/fedgov.html*

Career Mosaic — *http://www.careermosaic.com*

Career Path — *http://www.careerpath.com*

Job Center — *http://www.jobcenter.com/team/emplinks.htm*

Other Federal Job Information Sources:

State Department Civil Service Jobline — (202) 647-7284

State Department Foreign Service Exam — (703) 875-7490

OPM Job Line — (202) 606-2700

Career America Connection — (912) 757-3000 — A telephone-based system offering current worldwide federal job opportunities; online information and application packages mailed to you; salaries and employee benefits information; special recruitment messages; and forms requests.

Federal Job Opportunities "Bulletin" Board (FJOB) — (912) 757-3100 — A computer-based system offering the same features as the Career America Connection described above. You need a computer, modem, and communications software.

Judicial Clerkships

American Bench (Forster-Long, Inc., annual editions). A complete directory of state and federal judges including biographical information and addresses. The information is listed alphabetically by state and includes a description of every state court system.

Behind the Bench: The Guide to Judicial Clerkships by Debra Strauss (BarBri, 2002). This guide discusses all aspects of clerkships and the work judicial clerks do, although it should be noted that the 2002 edition was released before changes in federal judges' hiring timelines. Author Debra Strauss has started a private website at *www.judicialclerkships.com* that offers additional advice and resources.

Federal/State Court Directory (WANT Publishing Co., annual editions). Directory information on the federal and state courts. Provides names, addresses, and phone numbers of federal court judges and clerks of court, circuit executives, court librarians, bankruptcy court judges, probation officers, U.S. attorneys, U.S. magistrates, state chief justices, and attorneys general.

Directory of State Court Clerks and County Courthouses (WANT Publishing Co., annual editions). Information about judiciary on the state and local levels.

Electronic Resource

https://lawclerks.ao.uscourts.gov — The Federal Law Clerk Information System provides free law clerk vacancy announcements and hiring information for federal law clerk positions nationwide.

Networking/Business Etiquette

Effective Networking: Proven Techniques for Career Success by
Venda Raye-Johnson (Crisp Publications, Inc., 1990).

Great Connections: Small Talk and Networking for Businesspeople
by Anne Baber and Lynne Wayman (Impact Publications,
1991).

*How to Work a Room: The Ultimate Guide to Savvy Socializing in
Person and Online* by Susan RoAne (Quill, 2000).

*It's Who You Know: The Magic of Networking in Person and on
the Internet* by Cynthia Chin-Lee (Bookpartners, Inc., 1998).

Letitia Baldrige's New Complete Guide to Executive Manners
(Simon & Schuster, Inc., 1993).

Network Your Way to Job and Career Success (2nd edition)
by Ronald L. Krannich and Caryl Rae Krannich (Impact
Publications, 1993).

*The First Five Minutes: How to Make a Great First Impression in
Any Business Situation* by Mary Mitchell with John Corr
(John Wiley & Sons, Inc. 1998).

Working with Emotional Intelligence by Daniel Goleman (Bantam
Books, 1998). This excellent study outlines the yardsticks
for professional success: self-awareness, self-confidence,
and self-control; commitment and integrity; the ability to
communicate and influence, to initiate and accept change.

Electronic Resources

Here are two simple Martindale-Hubbell searches you can
perform on **LexisNexis**® to find alumni from your college or law
school. Alumni can be helpful resources for making initial contacts
based on school affiliation. The search segments are "college"
and "law-school." If you want to try to track down people with
similar language skills or who were born in a particular place,
consider searching by "languages" or "born." For more information
about career searching on LexisNexis, call 1-800-45-LEXIS.

You can also use the Internet to search the Martindale-Hubbell Lawyer Locator database by accessing *www.martindale.com*. Note, however, that the Internet version of Martindale-Hubbell is more limited than the LexisNexis text version that includes a greater array of search segments. For example, you can only search by law school affiliation, not college.

West Group also provides a searchable database containing potential networking leads based on college or law school affiliation, firm size, or practice area. To access this information, log on to West and access the West Legal Directories (WLD). West Legal Directories permit searches by lawyer name, state, area of practice, languages, firm size, law school, and college, among others. For more information about networking using Westlaw® databases, call 1-800-688-6363.

The following Internet sites offer information-gathering opportunities for law students and lawyers:

www.abanet.org/careercounsel — American Bar Association's career website. Enhance your networking and information-gathering potential by visiting the ABA's comprehensive listing of specialty sections, divisions, and forums at *www.abanet.org/sections.html.*

www.eAttorney.com — Martindale-Hubbell's eAttorney connects law students, attorneys, law schools, and law firms.

http://emplawyernet.com — Job opportunities and career development site for the legal community. This is a fee-based service. If your law school belongs to emplawyernet, then you may be eligible for discounted membership rates.

http://careers.findlaw.com — Job postings for lawyers, as well as career information.

www.hg.org/employment.html — Part of the Hieros Gamos site. Outstanding resource.

www.jurist.law/pitt.edu — The renowned University of Pittsburgh website with cutting-edge news and information related to the practice of law.

www.lawcrossing.com — A subscription service providing job listings culled from websites, employers, and legal publications throughout the U.S.

www.lawyers.com — "Find a Lawyer Quick Search" enables law students to conduct research by state, city, and practice area, although searches cannot be limited by firm size.

http://lawmatch.com — Résumé bank and job posting service that matches attorneys and other legal professionals with industry employers and recruiters. Free for Basic Service, fee for expanded services.

http://lawschool.westlaw.com/career/ — Attorney jobs and summer legal employment guide available through Westlaw.

www.lawyersweeklyusa.com — *Lawyers Weekly USA*, "The National Newspaper of Small Firms," offers articles about small firm practice and job postings.

http://legalemploy.com — The Legal Employment Search lists various sites that have legal job listings.

www.lawforum.net/index.html — The Law Forum is an online directory of law firms, legal support services, legal resources, legal employers, and more.

www.lawjobs.com — Jobs updated daily from a national network of legal newspapers and jobs updated weekly by top legal recruiters.

www.ljx.com/nlj — *The National Law Journal* offers breaking news and features, as well as salary surveys.

www.nalp.org — The official website of NALP — The Association for Legal Career Professionals — with detailed information about recruiting, hiring, and retention of lawyers, both entry-level and laterally, as well as an online catalog of law career-related publications available from NALP.

www.nationjob.com/legal — Legal and legal-related positions through nationjob.com.

www.palidan.com — Resources for lawyers and law students including links to other employment sites.

www.wetfeet.com — A good source for large firm research and overall industry information. Particularly helpful for nontraditonal job seekers.

Nontraditional Options

Beyond L.A. Law: Break the Traditional "Lawyer" Mold compiled by Janet Smith (NALP/Harcourt Legal & Professional Publications, Inc., 1998). Inspiring stories of people who have done fascinating things with a law degree.

Nonlegal Careers for Lawyers by Gary A. Munneke and William D. Henslee (American Bar Association Career Series, Law Student Division, 2003).

The Lawyer's Career Change Handbook: More Than 300 Things You Can Do With a Law Degree by Hindi Greenberg (Avon, 1998).

What Can You Do With A Law Degree: A Lawyer's Guide to Career Alternatives Inside, Outside & Around the Law by Deborah Arron (DecisionBooks, 2004). A classic on alternative careers for lawyers, full of excellent lists and resources. The publisher's website (*www.decisionbooks.com*) includes useful information on self-assessment tools, career counselors, and more.

Should You Really Be a Lawyer? The Guide to Smart Career Choices Before, During & After Law School by Deborah Schneider and Gary Belsky (DecisionBooks, 2004).

Practice of Law/Practice Subspecialties

The American Bar Association (ABA) General Practice, Solo and Small Firm Section provides information and assistance to lawyers in general practice, solo, and small firm settings. Lawyers who are members of the ABA can join the Section for $35. In addition to publications and newsletters, the Section conducts four quarterly meetings that provide opportunities for gaining CLE credit, networking with colleagues, and enjoying special events. For more information, e-mail *genpractice@abanet.org*.

From Law School to Law Practice: The New Associate's Guide (2nd edition) by Suzanne B. O'Neill and Catherine Gerhauser Sparkman (ALI/ABA, 1998).

Guerrilla Tactics for Getting the Legal Job of Your Dreams by Kimm Alayne Walton (Harcourt Legal & Professional Publications, Inc., 1999).

How to Start and Build a Law Practice (5th edition) by Jay G. Foonberg (American Bar Association, 2004).

The Official Guide to Legal Specialties: An Insider's Guide to Every Major Practice Area (BarBri/NALP, 2000). Incorporating interviews with 130 attorneys from private law firms of all sizes, solo practitioners, public interest organizations, and government agencies, this book offers insights on the nature of day-to-day work in 30 different practice areas.

What Law School Doesn't Teach You...But You Really Need to Know by Kimm Alayne Walton (BarBri, 2000). Expert tips and strategies for making your legal career a huge success from the author of *Guerrilla Tactics*.

Public Interest

There are many excellent directories focusing on public interest practice. Since many public interest efforts are local, you should consult your area bar association and career services office for information. The following are some printed resources that provide current information:

Private Public Interest and Plaintiff's Firm Guide (a joint publication of the Center for Public Interest Law at Columbia Law School and the Bernard Koteen Office of Public Interest Advising at Harvard Law School, 2004). This directory lists private public interest law firms — many small in size — throughout the U.S. Listings include firm names, locations, websites, types of advocacy, and contact information. Your career services office library should have this guide.

Public Interest Profiles (Congressional Quarterly & The Foundation for Public Affairs, annual). An in-depth guide to the most influential public affairs groups in the United States.

Making a Living While Making a Difference: A Guide to Creating Careers with a Conscience by Melissa Everett (Bantam Books, 1999). A general guide to careers based on individual values and public service.

Internet Resources

Two excellent websites for public interest jobs are:

Equal Justice Works (formerly The National Association for Public Interest Law) (**www.equaljusticeworks.org**) was founded in 1986 by law students dedicated to surmounting barriers to equal justice that affect millions of low-income individuals and families. Today, Equal Justice Works leads the country in organizing, training, and supporting public service-minded law students, and in creating summer and postgraduate public interest jobs. Through more than $8 million in annual donations from law firms, corporations, foundations, individuals, and the federal government, Equal Justice Works funds law students and lawyers in programs that bring justice to millions of low-income persons and families.

PSLawNet (**www.pslawnet.org**), NALP's Public Service Law
Network Worldwide, serves as a comprehensive clearinghouse
of public interest organizations and opportunities for law
students and law graduates. Through its online database,
PSLawNet users can perform customized searches of public
interest opportunities around the world, ranging from short-
term volunteer and paid internships to full-time jobs, fellowships, and *pro bono* opportunities. PSLawNet's database currently includes more than 12,000 law-related public interest
organizations in the U.S. and around the world.

Salary Information/Negotiation

Associate Salary Survey (NALP, annual) — an excellent resource
for data regarding associate salaries nationally, regionally, by
firm size, by metropolitan area size, by year of graduation,
and for particular cities. Your career services office should
have at least one copy of this resource. If you would like to
order your own, contact NALP at (202) 835-1001 or visit
NALP's online bookstore at *www.nalp.org*.

*Dynamite Salary Negotiations: Know What You're Worth and Get
It* by Ronald L. Krannich and Caryl Rae Krannich (Impact
Publications, 4th Edition, 2000).

Getting to Yes: Negotiating Without Giving In by Roger Fisher
and William Ury (Penguin USA, 1991).

IOMA's Report on Compensation and Benefits for Law Offices is
a monthly publication of the Institute of Management &
Administration containing timely information about salaries
at law firms, benefits, and other relevant information. Either
your career services office or law library should carry this
publication. For ordering information, access *www.ioma.com*
or call (212) 244-0360.

Of Counsel: The Legal Practice and Management Report is published monthly by Aspen Publishers. It contains helpful information about associate hiring at large, mid-sized, and small
firms as well as regional markets. Either your career services
office or law library should carry this publication. For ordering
information, call (212) 597-0200 or visit Aspen's website at
www.aspenpublishers.com.

NALP Principles and Standards

Working together, the members of **NALP — The Association for Law Schools and Legal Employers** — developed ethical guidelines called the *Principles and Standards for Law Placement and Recruitment Activities*. The *Principles and Standards* define the responsibilities of law schools, candidates, and employers during the law student recruitment process and are particularly targeted to the fall "recruiting season," when many large law firms interview on-campus.

The *Principles and Standards* are revised from time to time to reflect changes in prevailing recruiting practices and schedules. The most frequently cited portion of the *Principles and Standards* is Part V, "General Standards for the Timing of Offers and Decisions." This section suggests how long employers should hold offers open as well as suggesting the maximum number of offers a student should hold. The *Principles and Standards* are designed to help students who are participating in on-campus interviews complete their schedules before being required to make a decision, while also helping to level the playing field for employers.

The full text of NALP's current *Principles and Standards*, as well as helpful summary information, can be found on NALP's website at **www.nalp.org**. It is important to note that these ethical guidelines apply specifically to law students. Moreover, they particularly address the timing of offers and decisions during the fall on-campus interviewing process and thus are most relevant to large firm hiring. The *Principles and Standards* acknowledge the fact that small firms must fill needs as they occur by stating (in Part V, A.6), "Employers having a total of 40 attorneys or fewer in all offices may be exempted from Paragraphs B and C below [regarding fall timelines] but should leave offers open for a minimum of three weeks." In addition, the *Principles and Standards* suggest (in Part V, A.1), "All offers to law students should remain open for at least two weeks after the date made unless the offers are made pursuant to paragraphs B and C below [about fall timelines], in which case the later response date should apply."

Sample Cover Letter #1:   Response to a Job Posting

1114 North 27th Street
Apartment #8B
Pleasantville, PA 19104
April 14, 2005

Samuel L. Moore, Esq.
Moore & Moore
3110 Grant Building
Pleasantville, PA 19104

Dear Mr. Moore:

The career services office at the University of Pleasantville School of Law posted a notice regarding a full-time associate position with Moore & Moore. I enclose a copy of my résumé for your consideration.

Working for a small law firm in Pleasantville that concentrates its practice on family law would enable me to work in an area of the law that interests me greatly while cultivating hometown contacts to build your firm's client base. I am currently taking "Advanced Issues in Family Law" and participate in our school's Family Law Clinic, where, under the supervision of Professor James Smith, I represent indigent clients seeking no-fault divorces. I enjoy working with clients and resolving difficult issues. This past semester, I appeared before Judge Harlan J. Jones of the Pleasantville Family Court Division and presented a motion for reconsideration of alimony; following oral argument, that motion was granted. I feel confident that I have the interest, skills, and motivation to succeed as a family law practitioner.

I look forward to speaking with you about my credentials and learning more about your associate position. Please contact me at (412) 566-6630 or student@lawschool.edu to schedule an interview. Thank you for your consideration.

Sincerely,

Jane Q. Student

Enclosure

Sample Cover Letter #2: Networking Lead (General)

1114 North 27th Street
Apartment #8B
Pleasantville, PA 19104

February 14, 2005

Samuel L. Moore
Moore & Moore
3110 Grant Building
Pleasantville, PA 19104

Dear Mr. Moore:

I graduated from Faber College in 2002 and currently attend the University of Pleasantville School of Law where I am a first-year law student. I earned my undergraduate degree in electrical engineering and I am told that patent law is a natural practice niche for someone with my credentials. Before I proceed in this direction, however, I am interested in speaking with patent attorneys so that I may better understand the practice area and its demands.

I would appreciate any advice you might be able to share about your career path in patent law. If you have time to share your expertise and knowledge, either by telephone, in person, or through e-mail, then I would be most grateful. While I have read about patent law extensively, I believe that meeting with a practitioner and asking questions will help guide me in my choice of practice area.

I can be reached at (412) 123-4567 or via e-mail at student@lawschool.edu if you would be willing to speak with me. Thank you in advance for your assistance.

Sincerely,

John Q. Student

Sample E-mail Correspondence:
Alumni Networking Contact (More Than One Contact)

Tip: If your research reveals several promising alumni contacts, you can write to these individuals as a group. Either type all of the names in the "To" section or cut and paste and address each of the e-mails individually.

To: Jane Jones jjones@smalllawfirm.com
From: John Q. Student student@lawschool.edu
Date;   March 15, 2005

Subject: Practicing Law in Pleasantville/Faber College

My name is John Q. Student and I graduated from Faber College in 2002. I currently attend the University of Pleasantville School of Law where I am a first-year law student. I earned my undergraduate degree in electrical engineering and I am told that patent law is a natural practice niche for someone with my credentials. Before I proceed in this direction, however, I am interested in speaking with patent attorneys so that I may better understand the practice area and its demands.

I would appreciate any advice you might be able to share about your career path in patent law. If you have time to share your experience and knowledge, either by telephone, in person, or through e-mail, then I would be most grateful. While I have read about patent law extensively, I believe that meeting with a practitioner and asking questions will help guide me in my choice of practice area.

I can be reached at (412) 123-4567 or via e-mail at student@lawschool.edu if you would be willing to speak with me. Thank you in advance for your assistance.

Sample Thank You Letter

Note: Thank you letters are typically typed on 8-1/2 x 11-inch paper and should be mailed immediately following your interview.

1114 North 27th Street
Apartment #8B
Pleasantville, PA 19104
April 14, 2005

Samuel L. Moore, Esq.
Moore & Moore
3110 Grant Building
Pleasantville, PA 19104

Dear Mr. Moore:

Thank you for taking the time to interview me for the associate position with Moore & Moore. I enjoyed learning more about your firm and the challenges you face representing small businesses in the region. I remain very interested in working for your firm and serving clients who seek high-quality legal advice.

As I emphasized during our meeting, I have a strong interest in corporate law and have taken nearly every course in corporate governance, tax law, and business strategy that the University of Pleasantville School of Law offers. My prior experience at Grey Hawk Industries, coupled with my law clerk experience at the U.S. Small Business Administration, would enable me to be an effective contributor to your firm from the beginning.

I appreciate the opportunity to speak with you and your colleagues about the possibility of working for Moore & Moore and look forward to hearing from you soon. I can be reached at (412) 123-4567 or student@lawschool.edu.

Sincerely,

Jane Q. Student

Sample Thank You: E-mail Correspondence

Note: It is appropriate to e-mail a thank you note following an interview, although some may prefer to type and mail a letter.

From: Jane Q. Student student@lawschool.edu
Sent: March 15, 2005
To: Jane Jones jjones@smalllawfirm.edu

Subject: Thank you

Thank you for taking the time to interview me for the associate position with Moore & Moore. I enjoyed learning more about your firm and the challenges you face representing small businesses in the region. I remain very interested in working for your firm and serving clients who seek high-quality legal advice.

As I emphasized during our meeting, I have a strong interest in corporate law and have taken nearly every course in corporate governance, tax law, and business strategy that the University of Pleasantville School of Law offers. My prior experience at Grey Hawk Industries, coupled with my law clerk experience at the U.S. Small Business Administration, would enable me to be an effective contributor to your firm from the beginning.

I appreciate the opportunity to speak with you and your colleagues about the possibility of working for Moore & Moore and look forward to hearing from you soon. I can be reached at (412) 123-4567 or student@lawschool.edu.

Jane Q. Student
1114 North 27th Street
Apartment #8B
Pleasantville, PA 19104

1114 North 27th Street
Apartment #8B
Pleasantville, PA 19104

June 7, 2005

Samantha L. Moore
Moore & Moore
3110 Grant Building
Pleasantville, PA 19104

Dear Ms. Moore:

Thank you for your offer of full-time employment as an associate with Moore & Moore. I am delighted to accept your offer and the terms upon which we agreed in our telephone conversation on June 6. As we discussed, I will begin work on September 6, 2005.

I appreciate your confidence in my abilities and look forward to using my skills as an attorney with your firm. Please call me if you have any questions or require additional information at (412) 321-7654. After August 1, I can be reached at (412) 123-4567.

I look forward to beginning work on September 6.

Sincerely,

Jane Q. Student

Sample Rejection Letter

1114 North 27th Street
Apartment #8B
Pleasantville, PA 19104

June 7, 2005

Samantha L. Moore
Moore & Moore
3110 Grant Building
Pleasantville, PA 19104

Dear Ms. Moore:

Thank you for your offer of full-time employment with Moore & Moore. Unfortunately, I have chosen to accept an offer elsewhere and, therefore, must regretfully decline your invitation to work at your firm.

Sincerely,

Jane Q. Student

LAURA GRAHAM
425 Sleepy Hollow Road
Apartment #5
Anyplace, PA 18104
(123) 456-7890
<u>graham@lawschool.edu</u>

EDUCATION

University of Columbia School of Law, Columbia, PA
J.D. expected, May 2005
Grade Point Average: 3.2/4.0   (Rank: 47/205)
- Teaching Assistant — Legal Writing & Research Class
- Member of the National Health Law Moot Court Team
- Semester Honors, Fall 2004
- Director of Bar/Bri Operations for the University of Columbia School of Law

University of Rhode Island, Kingston, RI
B.A. in Political Science, May 2002
B.S. in Consumer Affairs, concentration in Health, May 2002

Universidad de Granada, Granada, Spain
Intensive Spanish language program, Summer 2001

EXPERIENCE

Department of the Attorney General, State of Rhode Island
Rule 9 Student Attorney, Criminal Division; District Court, Juvenile, and Domestic Violence Units, Providence, RI, Summer 2004
- Represented the State of Rhode Island in criminal proceedings in District and Family Court.
- Researched family law and criminal matters pertaining to alimony, protection from abuse, and custody of minor children.
- Interviewed victims and witnesses and assisted in hearings.

Medical Health Association of America
Legal Extern, Division of Legislative Counsel, Washington, D.C., Summer 2003
- Analyzed major health care legislation, attended congressional hearings, and drafted comments in accordance with MHAA

policy on issues including: The Patient's Bill of Rights, cloning and stem cell research, and regulatory reform measures.

- Conducted legal research to substantiate MHAA policy on various issues and to refute contradictory assertions regarding the impact of pending legislation.
- Worked closely with congressional and federal lobbyists and created advocacy materials to assist in the advancement of the MHAA's legislative agenda.

OTHER

Enjoy playing golf, tennis, and squash.

(This would be a one-page résumé when prepared on 8½ x 11-inch paper.)

JUNEKAWNG (JANE) TAE
3110 Centre Avenue, Apt. 3B
Mercer, PA 15232
janetae@yahoo.com

EDUCATION

University of Pleasantville School of Law
Pleasantville, PA
J.D. candidate, May 2006
     Asian Law Students Association, Vice President (2005)

Korea University, Seoul, Korea
B.A. in Philosophy, 2000
     Recipient of Korea University Scholarship (1998–2000)

LEGAL EXPERIENCE

Research Assistant (May – August 2004)
Professor Jones, University of Pleasantville School of Law
Researched Chinese law regarding taxation of nonprofit organizations
and the economic theory of a transition economy in China.
Wrote memorandums with respect to transitional fiscal reforms of
European and South American countries in contrast to the Chinese
economic model.

Summer Associate (May – August 2003)
Yoon and Partners, Seoul, Korea
Researched Korean law on foreign direct investment and the
establishment of branch offices, as well as corporations, in Korea
by foreign entities. Translated patent documents, statutes, and
contracts from Korean to English. Researched prior use of patented
product through the U.S. Patent and Trademark Office.

OTHER EXPERIENCE

Targaman Industries (2000–2003)
Management Training Program, Human Resources Division,
Denver, CO
Served as management trainee and Assistant Director of Human
Resources for regional manufacturing concern with headquarters in

Denver and subsidiaries through Southeast Asia. Worked closely with General Counsel and Assistant General Counsel to ensure compliance with applicable federal, state, and other employment law regulations.

SKILLS/INTERESTS

Fluent in Korean and English
Skiing, playing guitar, and opera

(This would be a one-page résumé when prepared on 8½ x 11-inch paper.)

MICHAEL T. BURTON
906 Maryland Avenue
Philadelphia, PA 19104
(610) 344-5678
mburton@aol.com

EDUCATION

University of Pleasantville School of Law, Pleasantville, PA
JD expected, May 2006
Civil Litigation Certificate Program
Litigation-Related Courses: Legal Research & Analysis (A–); Complex
Litigation (B+); Trial Advocacy (A–); Class Action Seminar (A+); and
Trial Advocacy Clinic (B+)
Activities: Student Bar Association, Class Representative, 2003–2004;
University of Philadelphia Chapter of American Inns of Court
(accepted for 2005–2006 academic year)

University of Maryland at College Park, Scholars' College,
College Park, MD
B.A. in Government and Politics, May 2003
Minor: Criminal Justice   Cumulative GPA: 3.45
Honor Societies: Omnicron Delta Kappa, Mortar Board, Order of
Omega, Maryland Medallion
Awards: Adele H. Stamp Award (finalist); Dean's List (Spring 2003,
Fall 2002, Fall 2001)

EXPERIENCE

Neighborhood Legal Services Association, Philadelphia, PA
Legal Practicum, Fall 2005

Poller, Bragg, Cummings & Glosser, LLC, Philadelphia, PA
Law Clerk, Summer 2005 – Present
  • Research and draft briefs, memoranda, petitions, and
    pleadings for small family law practice
  • Attend and assist with attorney-client conferences, settlement
    meetings, and court proceedings

Undergraduate Student Legal Aid Office, University of Maryland
Student Defender, August 2002 – May 2003
- Provided advice and direction for students charged with disciplinary or scholastic misconduct
- Appeared as student advocate at campus judicial hearings
- Authored opening statements, closing arguments, and appeals on behalf of student clients

Office of the District Attorney, Philadelphia, PA
Undergraduate Intern, May 2001 – August 2001
- Researched and briefed *habeas corpus* cases in Third Circuit courts for the appellate division

(This would be a one-page résumé when prepared on 8½ x 11-inch paper.)

About the Author

Donna Gerson is a contributing editor for *Student Lawyer Magazine*, an American Bar Association publication, and the author of numerous articles and brochures on legal career issues.

She served as the director of the career services office at the University of Pittsburgh from 1994–2001. Prior to her work in career services, Gerson clerked for a judge and worked in private practice.

Gerson is a member of the American Bar Association, the Pennsylvania Bar Association, and the Allegheny County Bar Association and is licensed to practice law in the Commonwealth of Pennsylvania.

Gerson earned her undergraduate degree from the University of Pennsylvania, her law degree from Temple University, and her master's degree in Library and Information Sciences (MLIS) from the University of Pittsburgh.

A popular speaker at law schools nationwide, Gerson lectures about small firm hiring practices, job seeking strategies for lawyers, and networking skills. She can be reached at *donna@donnagerson.com*.

About NALP

**NALP — The Association for Legal Career
Professionals** — is a nonprofit alliance of law schools
and legal employers. Founded in 1971 as the National
Association for Law Placement, NALP is committed to
the mission of providing preeminent leadership and
expertise in legal career planning, recruitment and
hiring, employment, and professional development
worldwide. To that end, NALP has published numerous
resources for job seekers as well as for career services
and legal recruitment professionals and also distributes
additional resources from other publishers. For information on resources currently available from NALP,
visit the online bookstore at **www.nalp.org**. NALP's
website also features research findings, including
national summaries of the annual NALP *Associate
Salary Survey*, and other information relevant to J.D.
job seekers.